From **GUIDING LIGHTS** to **BEACONS** for **BUSINESS**

THE MANY LIVES OF MAINE'S LIGHTHOUSES

EDITED BY RICHARD CHEEK

INTRODUCTION BY
SENATOR OLYMPIA J. SNOWE

WITH ESSAYS BY
W. H. BUNTING, RICHARD CHEEK,
THOMAS ANDREW DENENBERG,
TIMOTHY HARRISON, KIRK F. MOHNEY,
DAVID RICHARDS,
AND EARLE G. SHETTLEWORTH, JR.

HISTORIC NEW ENGLAND

Boston 2012

BOON ISL. LIGHT

VINEYARD SOUND

Two Fixed White · Steam Whistle ·

OWLS HEAD LIGHT

MATINICUS ROCK LIGHT

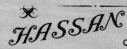

GOAT ISL. LIGHT

Contents

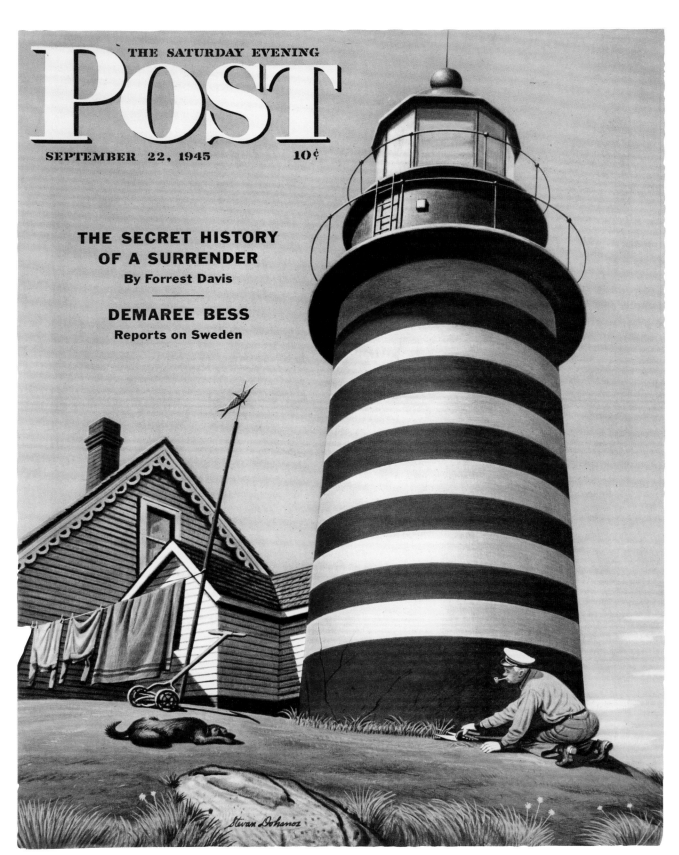

THE SATURDAY EVENING

POST

SEPTEMBER 22, 1945   10¢

THE SECRET HISTORY OF A SURRENDER
By Forrest Davis

DEMAREE BESS
Reports on Sweden

Stevan Dohanos. *Saturday Evening Post*. September 22, 1945.

Foreword

Popular interest in aspects of American and New England history rises and falls with changing times. Patriotic sentiment in the bicentennial years led to the creation of local house museums. Social change in the 1960s and 1970s generated a focus on ethnic and immigrant history. Increasing diversity of thought opened the new social history, with emphasis on everyday lives and working-class stories. Through all of these economic, political, military, and social approaches to the past, interest in the lighthouse has been uniquely consistent. Although these beacons are part of everyday experience only for the few people who work in them or live nearby, fascination with lighthouses touches millions, from student and scholar, writer and painter, architect and decorator. New England's extensive coastline and important harbors have made the region a place for lighthouses throughout three centuries.

In this volume we turn to ephemera collections to explore the many aspects of lighthouse history and lore. The trustees and staff of Historic New England are committed to using our historical collections to open windows into New England's rich heritage. We are grateful to Series Editor Richard Cheek, whose own appreciation for visual history sparked and guides our continuing effort to look at our collections with fresh eyes and to explore new themes that are of interest not only to the scholar, but to everyone. We thank Senator Olympia J. Snowe for her introduction and our friends at Maine Preservation, an organization that promotes an appreciation of Maine's historic places, their preservation, and use, for working with Historic New England to fund creation of this book. Lorna Condon and the staff of our Library and Archives devoted endless hours to this project, and did so with unfailing patience and enthusiasm for sharing historical resources through sound scholarship and lively and fun illustrations and design. The authors each bring special expertise and distinct individual approaches to lighthouse history that reveal the seemingly innumerable ways in which lighthouses appear in our lives. We thank them for their contributions. Ultimate thanks, however, is reserved for those members, friends, donors, and supporters of Historic New England who for more than one hundred years have helped create our collections, care for them, and make them available to you and to all through projects such as this. These efforts are about the past, but for the future.

Carl R. Nold

President and CEO

HISTORIC NEW ENGLAND

Boston, Massachusetts

Editor's Note

Work on this book began twenty-four years ago when Earle G. Shettleworth, Jr., director of the Maine Historic Preservation Commission, asked his staff member, Kirk Mohney, to start research for an architectural history of Maine's lighthouses. The book was to be illustrated by a newly commissioned set of photographs taken in accordance with the standards of the Historic American Buildings Survey, which required the use of a view camera to produce 4 × 5 inch black-and-white negatives for deposit in the Library of Congress.

As the photographer fortunate enough to receive this commission, I was aware that the market for lighthouse books was already saturated with glossy color publications, and I wondered how well a black-and-white architectural history would do against such competition. My doubts made us pause after the photographs were taken to see if we could develop a more comprehensive and widely appealing approach, extending in many directions beyond the design and construction of the lights, but the gestation period took much longer than we anticipated. We envisioned a book that would examine all of the major roles that lighthouses have played in the lives of those who have come into contact with them, not just mariners, but authors, artists, photographers, businessmen, religious leaders, tourists, children, and the men and women responsible for keeping the lights or for preserving the stations for posterity.

It wasn't until Historic New England launched its visual history series in 2006 with *The Camera's Coast: Historic Images of Ship and Shore in New England* that we finally found the popular educational focus and flexible format that we had been looking for. *From Guiding Lights to Beacons for Business: The Many Lives of Maine's Lighthouses* now becomes the third volume in the series, with ten chapters written by seven authors. As Series Editor, I am indebted to the scholars who joined Earle, Kirk, and me in examining the different facets of Maine's colorful lighthouse history with such clarity and enthusiasm: Bill Bunting, Tom Denenberg, Tim Harrison, and David Richards.

The dynamic layout of this book is due to the creative eye of the series' designer, Julia Sedykh. Historic New England's Senior Curator of the Library and Archives Lorna Condon shepherded the complicated production process from start to finish with her usual calm but exacting attention to detail, aided once again by our publishing consultant, Steve Pekich, and our legal advisor, Jeff Johnson of WilmerHale. Lorna's colleagues, Jeanne Gamble and Jennifer Pustz, succeeded in keeping track of the hundreds of images that were assembled for the book and in obtaining the necessary scans and permissions for reproduction. We also profited from the addition of two new members to our crew, Justin Goodstein-Aue, who took great pleasure in digitally photographing the never-ending stream of illustrations for the book, and Jim Mooney, who expertly edited our "p"s and "q"s.

Historic New England's series would not be possible without the generosity of thoughtful donors and the whole-hearted support of President Carl R. Nold, whose watchful eye over the project is as dependable as a light keeper's.

Having the excuse to search for rare or unusual illustrations at ephemera shows and antiquarian book fairs was the special joy of being this book's editor. I was greatly assisted by the knowledge and advice of many dealers and collectors, especially James W. Claflin, but I have to admit that someone else had already done a great deal of the lighthouse image hunting before I got started. Over the last twenty years, Tim Harrison, editor of *Lighthouse Digest* and one of our authors, has assembled the mother lode of lighthouse imagery and ephemera, now located in Whiting, Maine. From historical photographs and documents to advertisements and shoulder patches—anything to do with light stations in Maine or elsewhere in the U. S.—he's got it, I borrowed it, and you'll see it in this book.

Richard Cheek, *Editor*

Each chapter has its own set of numbered illustrations, beginning with its frontispiece. When several images appear on a page, they are numbered from left to right and then top to bottom. For additional information, see Illustration Sources, Endnotes, and Bibliography at the back of the book.

Introduction

Our great state of Maine is blessed with many beloved icons; among their ranks, standing tall along our shores for nearly two centuries, have been our state's legendary lighthouses.

Every lighthouse tells a different and unique story, and each one is as integral to the history and narrative of our state as the magnificent landscapes on which they proudly stand. How appropriate it is, then, that this third volume in Historic New England's series offers a stunning visual history of our lighthouses and takes us on an inspired journey of these remarkable Maine landmarks, rich in American maritime history, culture, and art.

As so many of the chapters of this book indicate, the lighthouse is truly one of the most American of symbols. It embodies our nation's enduring sense of resilience, rugged individualism, and concern for the common good. I cannot help but consider the solitary lives of countless lighthouse keepers who of their own volition bore tremendous burdens and responsibilities often fraught with the perils of life and death in order to help mariners reach the shore safely.

Not surprisingly, the lighthouse has also captured the imagination of many American painters, including Edward Hopper and Jamie Wyeth. Both of these giants of American art shared longtime associations with our state—as Jamie Wyeth still very much does—and painted well-known works depicting lighthouses in Maine. In fact, I have a print of Jamie Wyeth's vivid *Iris at Sea* in my U. S. Senate office.

The lighthouse also stirred renowned American poets like Maine's own Henry Wadsworth Longfellow, who characterized a lighthouse as being "steadfast, serene, immovable, the same/Year after year, through all the silent night/Burns on forevermore that quenchless flame,/Shines on that inextinguishable light!"[1] A native of Portland, Longfellow was likely moved to write those words by one of Maine's most famous lighthouses, the majestic Portland Head Light.

Symbolic of our state's seafaring history, the stately treasures that dot our coasts were indeed sturdy, dependable, and constant and could withstand all of the elements that Nature could muster—high winds, torrential rains, crashing waves, and impenetrable fog. They also spoke to an integrity of purpose, unassailable work ethic, and independence borne out of the courage to stand alone—traits that have always been indicative of the bedrock character and unshakable strength of our great state of Maine.

As you can imagine, as a Maine Senator, I have always been a strong champion of preserving these historic emblems. In fact, in my first year in the Senate, I introduced a bill that would later become law to establish the Maine Lights Program. We succeeded in conserving this vital component of American heritage through collaboration among the federal government, the state of Maine, local communities, and private organizations.

As this book makes clear, lighthouses are vital pillars of Maine's heritage and tourism industry, which contributes to the overall economic vitality of myriad Maine businesses. The Maine Tourism Association has said that "lighthouse history and preservation is a key component of Maine tourism," and I couldn't agree more. And the visitors' center in the Penobscot Bay region alone attracts nearly sixty thousand visitors per year, where the primary question that's asked is, "where can we see lighthouses in the area?"

It's been said that for a ship that has set sail, a fallen lighthouse is more dangerous than a reef—that is how indispensable these instruments of navigation and safety have been down through the ages, and continue to be today, historically, culturally, and economically. And how could it be otherwise as these structural gems are woven intricately into the fabric of Maine, New England, and, indeed, the nation.

Thank you for allowing me to share my thoughts with you on such an extraordinary endeavor. We owe a profound debt of gratitude to all who have been instrumental in bringing this outstanding project through to fruition. These beacons have long been our protectors —it's only fitting that we should also be theirs.

Olympia J. Snowe, *United States Senator*

"THE HURRICANE"

MARCH-TWOSTEP.

BY
S. L. ALPERT
ARRANGED
BY
E.T. PAULL

PUBLISHED BY **E.T. PAULL MUSIC C.O** 46 WEST 28th ST.

PHILADELPHIA, PA.
M. D. SWISHER.

SPRINGFIELD, MASS.   PHILADELPHIA, PA.
A. H. GOETTING.   JOS. MORRIS.

NEW YORK.
NEW YORK MUSIC SUPPLY CO.

NEW YORK
NEW YORK.
CROWN MUSIC CO.
NEW YORK.
ENTERPRISE MUSIC CO.
COPYRIGHT FOR ALL COUNTRIES.

LONDON, ENG.
W. PAXTON & C.o

CHICAGO, ILL.
F. J. A. FORSTER C.o

TORONTO, CAN.
CANADIAN-AMERICAN MUSIC CO. LTD.

BOSTON, MASS.
COUPON MUSIC CO.

(5) PIANO SOLO
(10) FOUR HAND
(4) SIMPLIFIED

Copyright
MCMVI.
By E.T. PAULL.

LITH. BY A. HOEN & CO. RICHMOND, VA.

Throw Out the Lifeline!

Wrecks and the Hazards of Coastal Navigation

W. H. Bunting

WRECK OF THE "BOHEMIAN" AS SEEN THE MORNING AFTER SHE SUNK.

2

On the night of February 22, 1864, the British mail steamer *Bohemian*, delayed several days by bad weather, arrived off Portland Harbor from Liverpool. The wind was calm, the sky overhead was clear, but a low fog obscured visibility, and the pilot schooner *Nettle* failed to see the steamer's signals requesting assistance. Aboard *Bohemian*, Captain Borland, no doubt weary and eager to land the mails without further delay, and expecting to see the light on Portland Head in good time, slowly stood in toward shore. When, at eight o'clock, *Bohemian* struck Alden's Rock, a buoyed reef two and a half miles east of Portland Head, Captain Borland thought his ship was still two miles farther offshore. Far worse for a navigator than knowing he didn't know where he was, was believing he was where he was not.

Bohemian, leaking badly, with over three hundred people and a cargo worth a million dollars on board, was promptly headed for shore. Lifeboats were launched, but one swamped in the process, throwing its occupants into the cold water with a heavy loss of life. The steamer ended up not on the shore, but partially submerged on the rocks in Broad Cove. The fisher folk of Cape Elizabeth, roused from their beds, rendered great aid to the freezing, bedraggled survivors. Forty of 199 immigrant passengers and two crew members died.[1] In 1865, in response to the tragedy, the tower of Portland Head Light was elevated and the power of the lantern increased.

The *Bohemian* disaster was typical of many Maine shipwrecks in that it began with fog and ended on a rocky ledge, and it was winter, the most dangerous season. But in some other respects it was unusual. While running aground on the infinitely complicated and tide-scoured

Drawn by W.K. Hewitt.   N. Currier, Lith & Pub. 2 Spruce St. N.Y.

Awful Conflagration of the Steam Boat **LEXINGTON** In Long Island Sound on Monday Eve⁰. Jan'. 13th 1840. by which melancholy occurrence ; over 100 PERSONS PERISHED.

Nathaniel Currier. *Awful Conflagration of the Steam Boat* Lexington. Undated.
Michele and Donald D'Amour Museum of Fine Arts,
Springfield, Massachusetts.

Maine coast under conditions of poor visibility was common, United States Life-Saving Service reports in the 1890s show that relatively few such events were fatal for vessels or for humans. Most vessels were refloated, thanks to the help of the local lifesavers who responded to disasters year round, even though stations were officially unmanned from May through August.

British mail steamers were found only at Portland, which served as Montreal's winter port via the Grand Trunk Railroad. In fact, aside from the regular Boston steamers and big multimasted coasting schooners bringing coal and often departing with ice, relatively few large vessels of any type were commonly found in Maine waters. Although many of the vast number of ships built in Maine were shipwrecked, most were lost elsewhere, often on some foreign reef or shore. And closer to home, surely many more Maine vessels—and sailors and fishermen—were lost on Cape Cod's beaches and associated bars, banks, and shoals, than on the rocky ledges of Maine. Cape Hatteras, as well, was another graveyard for Maine ships. In easterly gales both sandy capes featured seemingly endless lee shores of pounding surf; by contrast the Maine coast (east of Cape Porpoise), for all its countless protrusions and impediments, offered numerous possible harbors of refuge. And sheltered behind Maine's seaward island ramparts were large bays which became the haunt of old schooners of the "apple blossom fleet"—named for the season of their annual appearance—that had become too ripe for open waters and had to live out their final years in tame domestic drudgery.

HARPER'S WEEKLY.

A JOURNAL OF CIVILIZATION.

VOL. XIX.—No. 961.]   NEW YORK, SATURDAY, MAY 29, 1875.   [WITH A SUPPLEMENT. PRICE TEN CENTS.

Entered according to Act of Congress, in the Year 1875, by Harper & Brothers, in the Office of the Librarian of Congress, at Washington.

JOURNAL EXTRA!

THE LATEST!

BY TELEGRAPH.

THE LOSS OF THE NARRAGANSETT.

About 100 Lives Reported Lost.

List of Passengers Saved and Taken to New York.

CK LIGHT.—DRAWN BY J. O. DAVIDSON.—[SEE PAGE 437.]

APPALLING DISASTER

ON

THE SOUND.

The Steamers Narragansett and Stonington Collide.

The Narragansett Takes Fire and is Sunk.

SAD LOSS OF LIFE.

The Number Lost Not Yet Definitely Known.

ARRIVAL OF SOME OF THE PASSENGERS IN BOSTON.

Their Statements, &c. ⸮

About 175 Persons Rescued by Other Vessels.

The Number of Passengers Believed to Have Been Over 300.

Post–Civil War Americans embraced death with a morbid fascination, even hanging prints of horrible disasters in the parlor. Every steamboat was a potential conflagration awaiting the ignition of an excelsior-stuffed mattress by a sleepy passenger's capsized pipe. Thanks to very good fortune and to alert night watchmen sniffing at stateroom doors, no Boston to Maine steamer burned up while underway.

THE DEPARTURE GOOD BYE.

HEAVING THE LEAD

NAVAL ENGAGEMENT

"WREC

A STORY

INCIDENTS IN

Ironically, this nautical extravaganza appeared in the same issue of *Harper's Weekly* that led with the story of the wreck of the *Bohemian*, offering a central image with an archaic merchant vessel in dire trouble. The naval Jack Tars pictured in the surrounding tableaus, like sailors in the American merchant marine, were mostly foreigners by this date. While no doubt some were met upon their return from a cruise by a doting wife and child, most made do with the brief and impersonal embrace of a professional greeter in a house of ill repute. (Fig. 7)

PORT

THE RETURN.

FURLING SAIL

ESCUE.

THE SEA,
LIFE OF A SAILOR.

BETWEEN DECKS

In addition to drowning, merchant sailors also commonly died from falls, tropical fevers, and so forth. The bodies of sailors were buried at sea, but the remains of captains and their wives were sometimes buried at the next port of call, or even brought home. In some instances a stone set in a family plot memorialized a missing mariner. For fishermen, drowning was indeed the prime hazard, with offshore vessel fishermen the most likely to be lost wholesale in a gale. (Figs. 8–12)

Society for the Relief of Destitute Children of Seamen

The Home at West New Brighton, Staten Island, N.Y. Visitors welcomed

BOARD OF COUNSELORS

MR. CHARLES H. MARSHALL
MR. WM. ALLEY BUTLER
MR. FREDERIC DE P. FOSTER
CAPTAIN G.D.S. TRASK
MR. GUY Æ. IRVING
CAPTAIN FRANCIS A. MARTIN
MR. VERNON H. BROWN

OFFICERS

MRS. NATHANIEL MARSH, 1st Directress
MRS. BLYNN C. WEBSTER, 2nd Directress
MRS. GUY Æ. IRVING, Treasurer
MRS. TILLOCK A. LEGGETT, Rec. Sec'y
MISS ADELE T. LOW, Cor. Sec'y

Capt.
ALLEN HODGDON
lost at sea
Dec. 10, 1857.
Æt. 37 yrs.

GRANVILL HODGDON
lost at sea
Dec. 10, 1857.
Æt. 24 yrs. 10 mos.

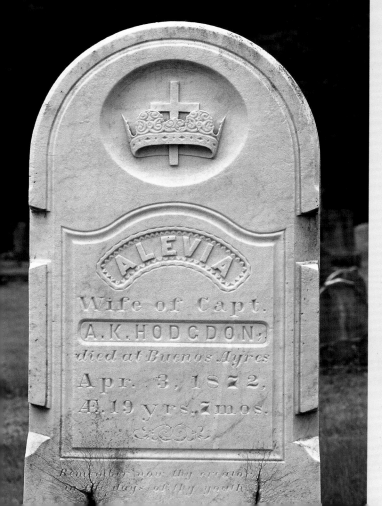

ALEVIA
Wife of Capt.
A.K. HODGDON,
died at Buenos Ayres
Apr. 3, 1872,
Æ. 19 yrs. 7 mos.

Remember now thy creator
in the days of thy youth

THE SAILOR'S FAMILY

13

Winslow Homer. *The Fog Warning*. 1885.
Photograph © 2012 Museum of Fine Arts, Boston.

A halibut fisherman on the off-shore banks hears a warning signal from his mother ship—the schooner seen on the horizon at right—as she races to retrieve her scattered dories before the fast-approaching fog bank to windward envelops all.

When a veteran coaster captain or fisherman looked out across a familiar body of water he "saw" as well the topography of the bottom. His leadline was among his most important tools of navigation, and his brain had filed away its many findings over the years. In 1895, Captain B. J. Willard, referring to Casco Bay fishermen of the 1840s, wrote: "At that time no compasses were used by the fishermen. They all went to any shoal they wished, steering by the sea. In thick fog a swell would roll in from the ocean, and the lead was used when near the shoal. Compasses were not employed til some of the boats got lost in a snow-storm coming home from White Head Grounds being misled by the changing of wind and no land in sight."[2]

Navigation in poor visibility required close attention and planning. Often the wisest course was to anchor first and ask questions later—as surely Captain Borland wished he had done. Fog built up on the eastern, windward sides of islands, so, ideally, one set a course for the western sides where the fog was likely to "scale up." Good hearing was important—different island bird colonies made different sounds. A bold headland echoed the bleat of the foghorn, although fog could muffle and deflect even the loudest of lighthouse steam-powered fog signals. A barking dog—especially if unexpected—always caught the navigator's attention. Smell could be an important indicator as well, as anyone passing to leeward of a dead-treed hangout of "shags," or cormorants, could attest.

14

15

OPERATION OF A SIREN (STEAM FOG-HORN)—SECTIONAL VIEW.

Mackerel seiners, their topsails sticking up through the low-lying summer fog, feel their way into Portland Harbor with the blink and bell of Ram Island Ledge Light ahead and to starboard. The view is from Cape Elizabeth. It is not surprising that mechanical means for ringing lighthouse fog bells were devised early on. Among the first lighthouses to be equipped with hot-air-powered Dabol trumpets were Portland Head Light and Manana Island Fog Signal Station, off Monhegan Island .

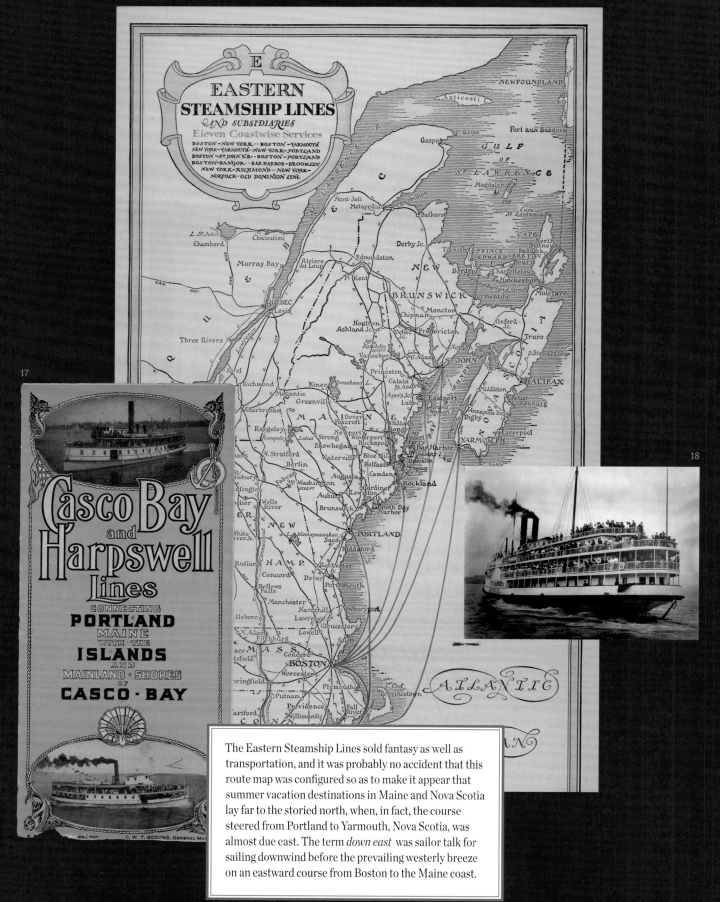

E

EASTERN
STEAMSHIP LINES
AND SUBSIDIARIES
Eleven Coastwise Services
BOSTON~NEW YORK ·· BOSTON~YARMOUTH
NEW YORK~YARMOUTH · NEW YORK~PORTLAND
BOSTON~ST JOHN N.B. · BOSTON~PORTLAND
BOSTON~BANGOR · BAR HARBOR~BROOKLIN
NEW YORK~RICHMOND · NEW YORK~
NORFOLK·OLD DOMINION LINE

The Eastern Steamship Lines sold fantasy as well as transportation, and it was probably no accident that this route map was configured so as to make it appear that summer vacation destinations in Maine and Nova Scotia lay far to the storied north, when, in fact, the course steered from Portland to Yarmouth, Nova Scotia, was almost due east. The term *down east* was sailor talk for sailing downwind before the prevailing westerly breeze on an eastward course from Boston to the Maine coast.

Coastal packet steamers, operating on regular routes, kept to their schedules despite poor visibility by timing runs on scores of memorized courses—many were but a matter of seconds in duration—calculating speed by engine revolutions. In confined waters, it was not unknown for a momentarily confused pilot to retrace his steamer's wake back to the last known position from which to take a fresh departure. Once in open water, to minimize the effects of tide and wind, steamer pilots were loath to slow down. So as not to "lose their place," as it were, they were reluctant to give way to, or steer widely around, blundering sailing vessels met in their path. Schooner captains, for their part, did not enjoy the close shaves or the possibility of being cut in half. Once, aboard a becalmed schooner whose tin foghorn had rolled off the railcap, pliers firmly applied to the tail of a crated pig produced a satisfactory warning to the fast-closing Bangor steamer.

In 1844, Captain William Flowers, of the Boston to Maine steamer *Huntress*, first ventured to take the "outside" route, rather than closely hugging the coast. By the 1850s, any vessel traversing the Maine coast would have had theoretically two major lighthouses in sight at all times, allowing for continuous fixes of position, but, of course, many a fogbank lay between theory and reality. Some of the many lighthouses that eventually marked the watery path to the booming summer resort of Mount Desert were testimony to the political influence of the steamboat lines and to Maine's powerful congressional delegation. The state emerged from the nineteenth century with perhaps the best-lit waters in the nation.

Steamers running from Boston to the shallow Kennebec and Penobscot rivers grew longer, wider, and higher, but not deeper. Such compromised creations had to be managed with great care on the open ocean portion of their route, from Cape Ann to Cape Elizabeth, or to Monhegan Island, the waypoint for steamers headed for Penobscot Bay.

The opportunities for disaster that daily presented themselves to a steamer pilot were manifold, and for every disaster that happened there were untold close calls. In September 1902, in the middle of a night thick with fog, the big Boston-Bangor steamer *City of Bangor*, filled with sleeping passengers, crept toward the faint and wavering sound of the powerful fog signal on Manana Island. Manana was the little sister to Monhegan, whose lofty lighthouse beacon was hidden by the vapor. Suddenly the dark mass of Monhegan itself loomed up right ahead as the steamer slid to a stop atop a ledge on that island's shore.

With no prospect of aid at hand, Captain Arey swallowed hard, backed his leaking steamer off the rocks, and made for Whitehead Light, sixteen miles away, posthaste, in a smother of rain. When off Spruce Head Island, with the water almost to the boiler fires, Captain Arey, still navigating in the dark, skillfully placed the steamer in a perfect mud berth atop the clam flats of Lobster Cove. The tide fell, the sun rose, and at daylight there the big steamer sat, high, dry, and safe (see above).

THE WRECK OF THE "ATLANTIC"—CAST UP BY THE SEA.—Drawn by Winslow Homer.—[See Page 342.]

20

Monhegan and Matinicus Rock, lying more than twenty miles to the east, were the gateposts for heavily traveled Penobscot Bay. North of Matinicus Rock, low-lying Matinicus and Ragged islands, ringed by smaller kin and breaking ledges and home to a prolific "fog factory," made for a very dangerous neighborhood from which a vessel that struck usually did not escape. Yet in the nearly one hundred years after the erection of the first lighthouse on "the Rock" in 1830, there were only about thirty wrecks in these waters. The islanders no doubt had mixed feelings about these slim pickings; bountiful wrecks were long remembered by the cargoes they had offered up.[3]

Pemaquid Point, lying about twelve miles northwest of Monhegan, separates John's Bay from Muscongus Bay. The lighthouse on Pemaquid stands as a warning, not welcoming, beacon, because often a very mean sea breaks at its feet on shelving rock and boulders. In 1635 the English ship *Angel Gabriel* was wrecked nearby in an August hurricane. Several of her hundred or so passengers died, while the survivors, with winter approaching, lost most of the essential supplies for their new lives in a strange wilderness.

In September 1903, the Gloucester mackerel schooner *George F. Edmunds*, seeking shelter in John's Bay during a strong onshore gale, went on the rocks just east of the lighthouse and quickly broke up. Fourteen of her sixteen-man crew were lost in the breakers. On the same day, the small coasting schooner *Sadie & Lillie* drove ashore on the west side of the point, tearing out her bottom. Two sailors survived, while her captain was drowned. Wreckage was strewn far along the shore.

The harsh reality of such a terrible day stood in bitter contrast to the romantic, melodramatic shipwreck nonsense served up by writers, artists, and illustrators of the period. Winslow Homer's print of a victim from the wreck of the *Atlantic* (above) and Henry Wadsworth Longfellow's popular poem "The Wreck of the Hesperus"[4] (at right) are typical examples. The corpses of freshly drowned maidens, garlanded with a lock of seaweed, looked nothing like the battered, bloated, eyeless remains of the lost husbands, fathers, and brothers that washed up with the tide on the rocks of Pemaquid.

At daybreak, on the bleak sea-beach,
   A fisherman stood aghast,
To see the form of a maiden fair,
   Lashed close to a drifting mast.

The salt sea was frozen on her breast,
   The salt tears in her eyes;
And he saw her hair, like the brown sea-weed,
   On the billows fall and rise.

Such was the wreck of the Hesperus,
   In the midnight and the snow!
Christ save us all from a death like this,
   On the reef of Norman's Woe!

THE WRECK OF THE HESPERUS

Romanticized shipwreck heroism notwith-standing, vessels were usually lost from mundane causes, or all-too-human lapses in judgment. For example, the song *The Ship That Sailed From Boston* was about the *City of Columbus* which struck a well-known shoal on a calm, clear night while on her regular run. A sailing ship's first voyage could well be her last if, shortly after putting to sea, she was caught in a powerful storm that stretched her new rigging excessively, result-ing in a cascading dismasting. Without the dampening effect of her top-hamper, a dis-masted ship rolled violently. (Figs. 24–30)

Today the wonders of electronic aids to navigation have taken most of the sport—the thrill of victory and the agony of defeat—out of coastal navigation. Although radar was long viewed as likely the last and best such invention, it has been eclipsed by compact GPS (Global Positioning System) devices that locate position and plot courses. Yet while the greenest of boaters can now boldly venture forth in the thickest of fogs, no such aid can be made foolproof; as has been proved, it is unwise to punch in a destination without first checking for intervening obstructions, such as islands. And going too fast with the GPS screen set at too close a range can have similarly disastrous results.

An experienced and careful navigator still intuitively and automatically double-checks the information provided by electronics with that from compass and eyeball. Lighthouses are still consulted. And on the Maine coast, but not along many southern New England shores, the distant beams and winks from lighthouses and buoys can still be picked up against the dark coastline, not yet having been overpowered by the loom and glare of cities and suburbs, of highways, malls, waterside condos, and other such achievements of our times.

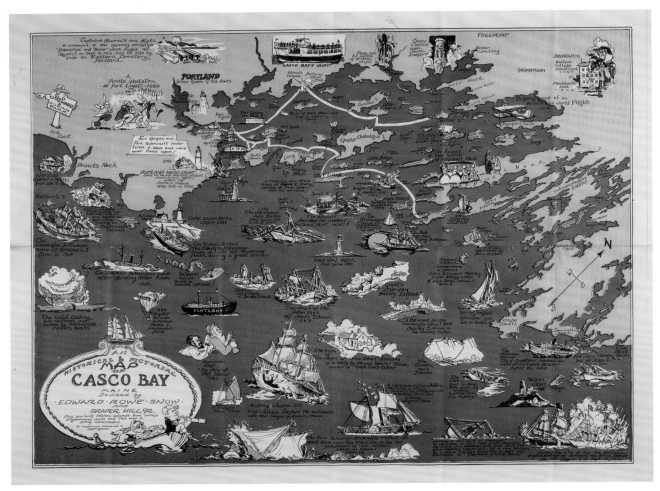

31

32

THIS IS COPY NUMBER *59* OF A SPECIAL AUTOGRAPHED EDITION CONTAINING FRAGMENTS OF WOOD FROM THE ILL-FATED STEAMER PORTLAND, WHOSE STORY IS TOLD IN THIS VOLUME.

Edward Rowe Snow

33

34

35

Edward Rowe Snow (1902–1982) was a colorful and original purveyor of coastal New England history who wrote many popular books, published lots of maps, and gave countless lectures. For successfully communicating his enthusiasm to a wide following, he deserved more credit than was sometimes accorded him by stuffy critics.

~ THE LIGHTHOUSE KEEPER'S SI

A. Emmanuelle Marpeau. *The Lighthouse Keeper's
Silent Conversation with the Sinking Ship*. 2001.

...VERSATION WITH THE SINKING SHIP ~

A shadow box fantasy by A. Emmanuelle Marpeau that is both playful and frightful. It brings to mind the terrible storm of November 1898 which sank the steamer *Portland*, drowning all on board. The packet schooner *Effort* survived the same gale by tacking back and forth in the lee of Manana Island as her captain's wife, on neighboring Monhegan Island, caught glimpses through the spindrift of the able little schooner's sails in the powerful beam of Monhegan's lighthouse.

1

Tower for Monhegan Light, Alexander Parris, 1849. This hand-colored rendering, prepared to show the architect's concept for the lighthouse, conveys the solidity and permanence of the proposed granite-block masonry. Parris introduced a level of sophistication to the design and construction of masonry light-house towers that had hitherto been lacking in Maine.

Shaping the Towers

The Architecture of the Lighthouses

Kirk F. Mohney

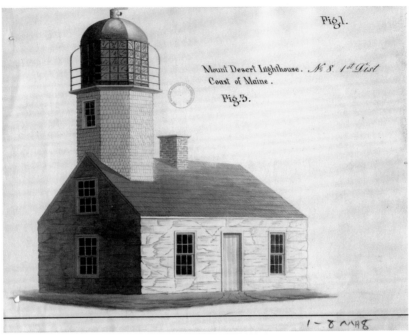

2

Lighthouse construction in Maine began with the erection of the Portland Head Light Station in 1790, more than half a century before the federal government was able to organize a systematic approach to the design of the towers. Hence, local craftsmen applied whatever existing building techniques seemed appropriate. When the United States Lighthouse Service finally did become involved in providing plans in the 1850s, constant experimentation and innovation caused frequent changes in the designs.

As a consequence, Maine's lighthouses are so varied in their method of construction and appearance that it is difficult to characterize them by architectural style. They differ in shape, size, building material, and finish. The towers are conical, cylindrical, rectangular, trape-zoidal, or octagonal. The tallest tower stands more than 130 feet from ground level to the top of its lantern, and the shortest is just over twenty feet. They may be built of brick, stone, wood, metal, or concrete. Most lighthouses are painted white, but some retain their natural stone color, others have black substructures and white superstructures, and one has alternating bands of white and red paint. With two exceptions, the towers support a glass-and-iron lantern room accessed by an interior staircase fashioned of stone, iron, or wood.

In this chapter, the term *lighthouse* refers to the structure that supports the lantern room, whereas the term *light station* means the entire complex of buildings and structures erected to support the maintenance of an aid to navigation at any given location.

Architectural photographs by Richard Cheek.

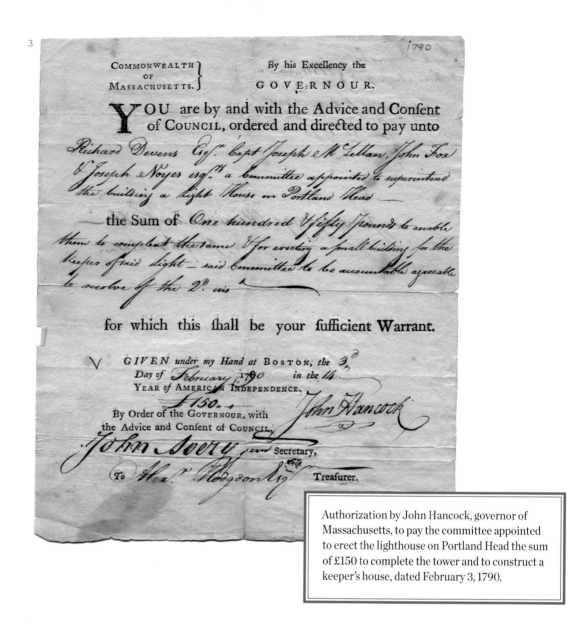

3

Authorization by John Hancock, governor of Massachusetts, to pay the committee appointed to erect the lighthouse on Portland Head the sum of £150 to complete the tower and to construct a keeper's house, dated February 3, 1790.

As Maine's first lighthouse, the Portland Head tower was built in conical form with rubble stone material, features that were to characterize most lighthouses erected before the middle of the nineteenth century. But a number of the earliest towers raised after Portland Head were octagonal structures or "pyramids" constructed of wood, including Seguin (1795), Wood Island, and West Quoddy Head (both 1808). It is noteworthy that the published specifications for the construction of a wooden tower on Whitehead Island in 1803 also requested "Terms . . . for building the Pyramid with good and suitable stone." Octagonal stone towers were subsequently constructed at Boon Island in 1811 and at Cape Elizabeth in 1828. Another configuration employed in the first half of the nineteenth century utilized a tower mounted atop the dwelling. At least four such lighthouses were known to have existed, but all of them were later replaced.

With only a few exceptions, lighthouse construction prior to the mid-nineteenth century appears to have been based solely on detailed specifications that were published in newspapers to solicit bids from contractors. No evidence has been discovered yet to indicate that trained engineers or architects were involved in the design of or drew plans for these early Maine lighthouses. As a result, craftsmen employing traditional methods of timber frame or rubble masonry construction created structures that were decidedly vernacular in form and appearance. This pattern changed in 1838 with the proposed reconstruction of the Whaleback Lighthouse (see page 34).

BURNT ISLAND (1821)

4

HABS NO. ME-212-6

WOOD ISLAND (1838)

5

PEMAQUID POINT (1835)

6

HABS NO. ME-123-20

MATERIAL: *Rubble Stone*

SHAPE: *Conical*

7

PORTLAND HEAD (1790, RAISED 1884)

ELEVATION
of
PROPOSED LIGHT HOUSE ON WHALE'S BACK
PORTSMOUTH HARBOUR.

Designed by Alexander Parris.
BOSTON

B

Elevation of Proposed Light House on Whale's Back,
Alexander Parris, 1838. Parris's striking concept for a
new lighthouse on Whaleback near the Maine/New
Hampshire border was not executed.

Perhaps because of the challenging site conditions, Alexander Parris of Boston, one of New England's most prominent architects, was engaged to design a replacement for the existing rubble masonry tower that had been standing on Whaleback since 1829. His concept for the granite lighthouse, which resembled John Smeaton's Eddystone Lighthouse in England (1759), was developed in several architectural drawings that show elevations, a section, and plans. Although Parris's design for Whaleback was not executed (the old tower remained in service until 1872), he subsequently drew the plans for seven lighthouses in Maine between 1839 and 1850, each of which was executed in ashlar masonry. They include the new lighthouse on Saddleback Ledge in 1839; the new tower on Mount Desert Rock, the reconstruction of the lighthouse on Matinicus Rock, and the new lighthouse at Little River, all in 1847; the new tower on Libby Island and the new lighthouse at Prospect Harbor, both in 1848; and the new tower at Monhegan Island in 1850. In addition, although erected after his death, the replacement tower built in 1852 at Whitehead appears to have been constructed from his plans for the Monhegan Island lighthouse. The design of the lighthouse at Matinicus Rock (see above) was distinguished by the twin towers integrated into the ends of the granite keeper's house. A similar relationship between tower and house was employed for the single lights at Little River and Prospect Harbor.

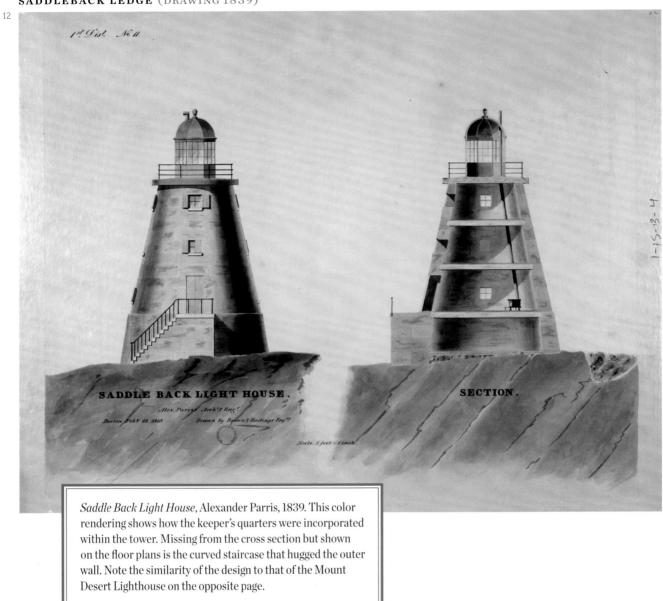

Saddle Back Light House, Alexander Parris, 1839. This color rendering shows how the keeper's quarters were incorporated within the tower. Missing from the cross section but shown on the floor plans is the curved staircase that hugged the outer wall. Note the similarity of the design to that of the Mount Desert Lighthouse on the opposite page.

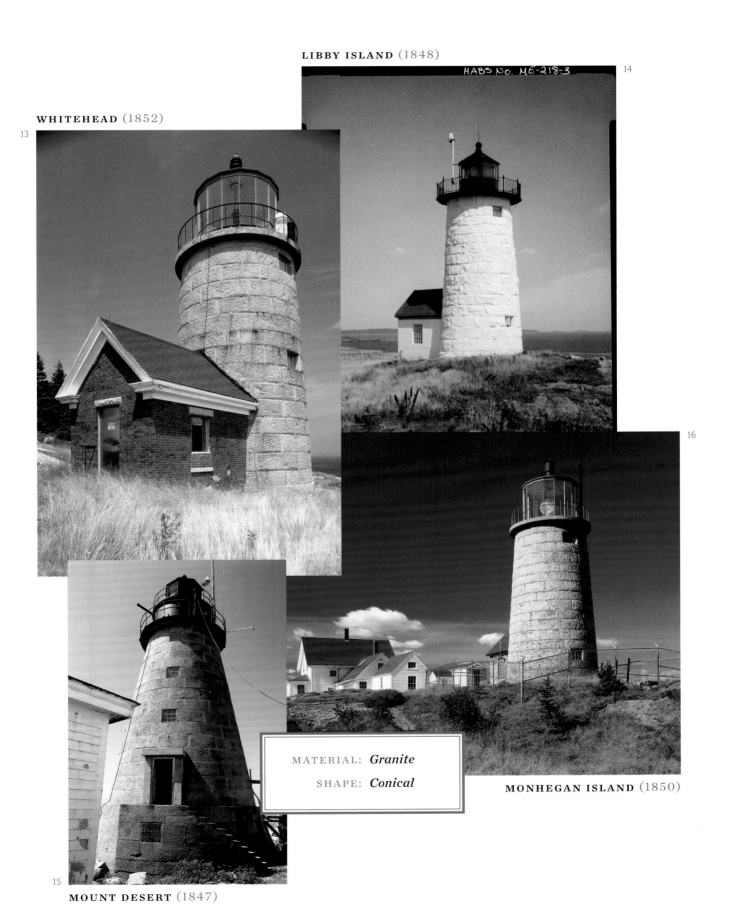

LIBBY ISLAND (1848)

HABS No. ME-218-3

14

WHITEHEAD (1852)

13

16

MATERIAL: *Granite*

SHAPE: *Conical*

MONHEGAN ISLAND (1850)

15

MOUNT DESERT (1847)

17

MATERIAL: *Granite*

SHAPE: *Conical*

Parris's work in Maine represents a bridge between the traditional building techniques that shaped the form and appearance of the early lighthouses and the professional architectural and engineering practices that were adopted as a result of the reorganization of the lighthouse establishment in the United States in 1852. The engineers assigned to the First Light House District were graduates of the United States Military Academy at West Point, who then were typically promoted into either the Topographical Engineers or the Corps of Engineers. Although they have been largely overlooked in most published lighthouse histories, it appears that they played a central role in shaping the distinctive architec-

tural character of the light stations. Their design skill is reflected in both architectural drawings and in the large number of lighthouses, keepers' houses, and other outbuildings that remain. During his tenure in the 1850s as the First Light House District inspector and engineer, Lieutenant William B. Franklin was involved with the reconstruction and establishment of many light stations. These projects ranged in scale from tall offshore granite towers to a series of modest board-and-batten wooden keepers' houses that were painted brown. His successors left their own distinctive mark on the design of Maine's lighthouses.

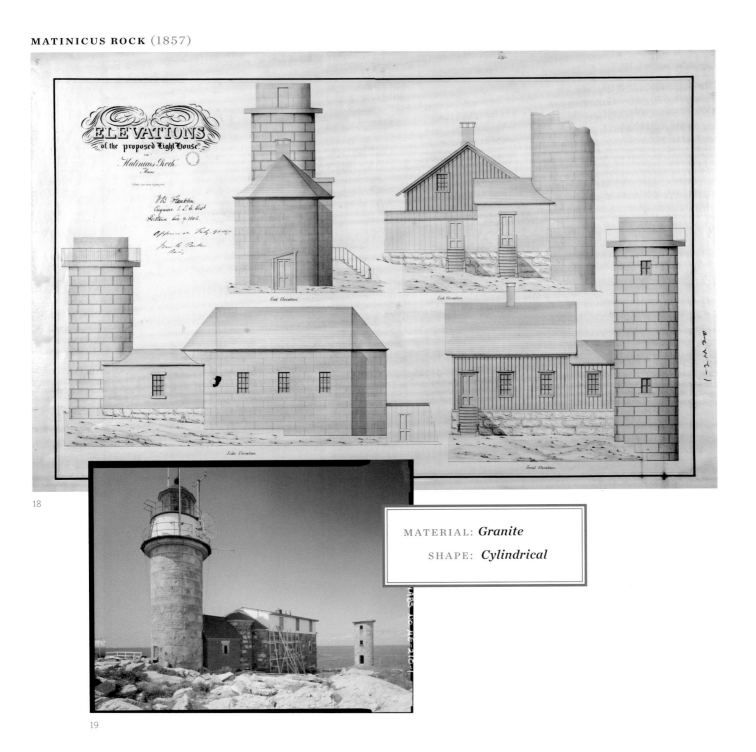

MATERIAL: *Granite*

SHAPE: *Cylindrical*

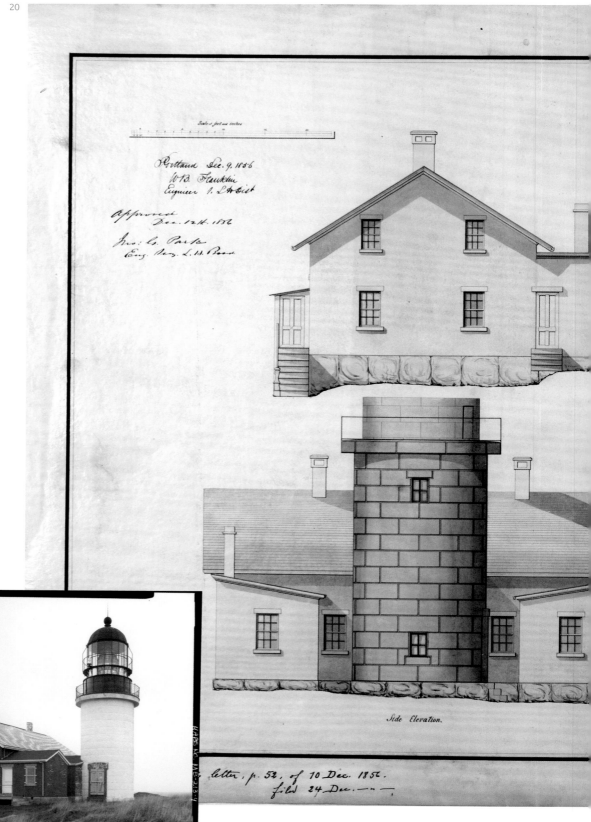

Side Elevation.

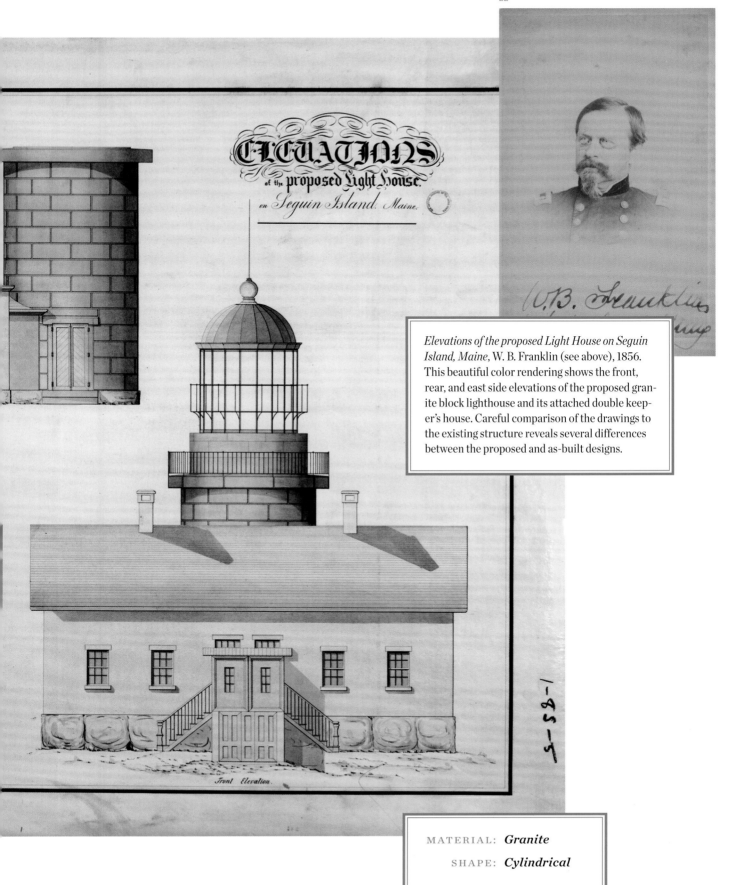

Elevations of the proposed Light House on Seguin Island, Maine, W. B. Franklin (see above), 1856. This beautiful color rendering shows the front, rear, and east side elevations of the proposed granite block lighthouse and its attached double keeper's house. Careful comparison of the drawings to the existing structure reveals several differences between the proposed and as-built designs.

MATERIAL: *Granite*

SHAPE: *Cylindrical*

PUMPKIN ISLAND (1855)

TENANT'S HARBOR (1858)

> MATERIAL: *Brick*
>
> SHAPE: *Conical & Cylindrical*

WEST QUODDY HEAD (1857)

26

The great period of construction and remodeling of Maine light stations that began in the 1850s saw a substantial change in both the design and materials used in lighthouses. The stone masonry that dominated the earlier period continued to be used in the most exposed locations, such as Boon Island and Petit Manan, where tall, nearly identical towers were erected in 1855. They were constructed of cut granite blocks, as were the new towers built in 1857 at Seguin and Matinicus Rock (two towers). But for the majority of new lights, smaller in scale and in more sheltered positions, brick emerged as the most popular building material, with the first such tower erected at Moose Peak in 1851. Both materials were employed in the 1857 replacement tower at Marshall Point, with brick used for the superstructure and cut granite blocks used for the base that stands in the tidal zone. To access this tower, a wooden truss bridge supported by three masonry piers was erected. Lighthouse design in the 1850s relied heavily on cylindrical forms, rather than the conical shape of the early towers, although rectangular towers were built at Fort Point and Deer Island Thoroughfare, both of which were erected in 1857.

Keeper's house, PROSPECT HARBOR

27

28

Oil house, WOOD ISLAND

29

30

Small boathouse, GREAT DUCK ISLAND

31

Boat winch, DOUBLING POINT

Bell house, HENDRICK'S HEAD

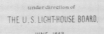

ELEVATIONS & OF

JONES' FOG-BELL,

ERECTED AT

CAPE ELIZABETH

under direction of
THE U.S. LIGHT-HOUSE BOARD.
JUNE 1888.

Bell house,
WHITLOCK'S MILL

Outbuildings were essential components of every light station in Maine except for the caisson type. The dwelling for the keeper, a privy, and an oil house might be accompanied by a boathouse, a bell house or fog signal building, a rain collecting shed, a fuel house, a wharf, a barn, a shed, and a henhouse. At Seguin a tramway, a coal bunker, a derrick, an engine house, and two reservoirs were constructed to support the fog signal.

34

Between 1870 and 1880 a number of light stations were either established or substantially rebuilt. The towers erected during this period exhibit continued experimentation with new shapes and materials. Three of them, including the newly built station at Burnt Coat Harbor (1872), as well as the rebuilt towers at Grindel Point and Indian Island (both in 1874), utilized a trapezoidal brick form, a tapered variation of the rectangular towers that first appeared in the 1850s. In 1875 a pair of light stations (Avery Rock and Egg Rock) were constructed with rectangular brick towers surrounded by one-story brick dwellings. Hooded, round-arched tower windows and darkly painted quoins imparted an Italianate style to the structures. The most significant technological innovation in lighthouse design in this period involved the use of prefabricated cast-iron plates

for tower construction. Employed at the twin towers at Cape Elizabeth (1874), the replacement lighthouse at Little River (1876), and the new light at Cape Neddick (1879), these handsome iron structures are among the most architecturally distinct of Maine's lighthouses, principally because of the Italianate-style ornamentation used above window openings and to support lantern decks. The ability to create decorative details in cast iron that could withstand the marine environment reached its greatest expression in the 1875 reconstruction of the Portland Breakwater Lighthouse, a striking design that was modeled after the fourth century B.C. Choragic Monument of Lysicrates in Athens. Also of special note was the use of grappier cement in the square base of the two towers at Cape Elizabeth, one of the first appearances of that material in Maine.

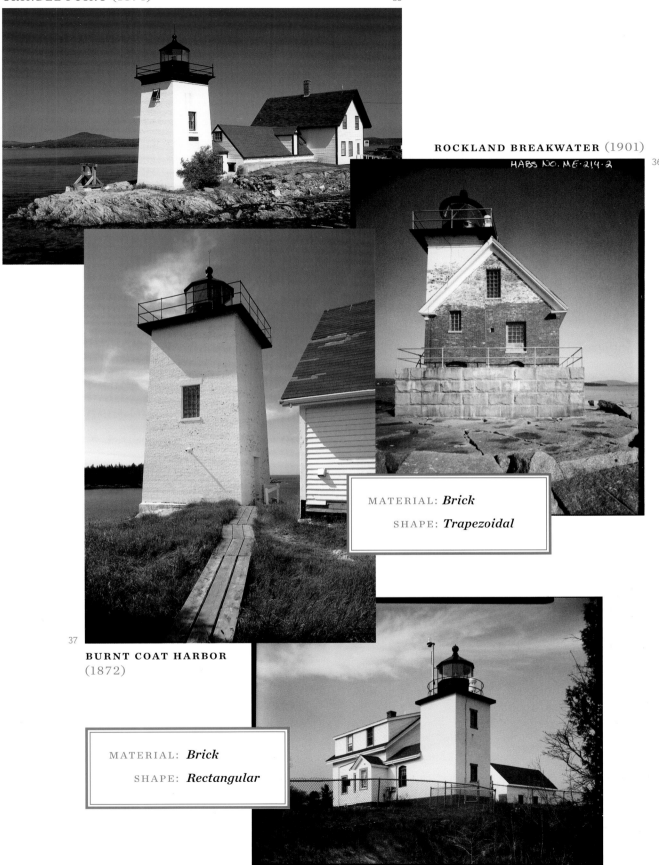

GRINDEL POINT (1874)

35

ROCKLAND BREAKWATER (1901)

HABS NO. ME·214·2

36

MATERIAL: *Brick*

SHAPE: *Trapezoidal*

37

BURNT COAT HARBOR
(1872)

MATERIAL: *Brick*

SHAPE: *Rectangular*

38

FORT POINT (1857)

MATERIAL: *Cast Iron*

SHAPE: *Conical & Cylindrical*

DOUBLING POINT FRONT RANGE (1898)   42

DOUBLING POINT (1898)

41

43

MATERIAL: *Wood*

SHAPE: *Octagonal*

SQUIRREL POINT (1898)

In the thirty years between 1880 and 1910, an additional fifteen light stations were established and four towers were replaced. Both the 1883 Ram Island lighthouse and the 1907 Isle Au Haut lighthouse (above) employed the same basic design concept that had been used at Marshall Point in 1857—complete with the wooden bridges. In 1890, three caisson-type lighthouses were built on Goose Rocks, in Lubec Channel, and on Crabtree Ledge. These identical structures featured a wide cast-iron-faced concrete substructure surmounted by a narrower cast-iron superstructure, the lower portion of which was sheltered by a gallery. The keeper's quarters and the storage facilities were contained within the tower. A variation on the design erected in 1897 at Spring Point Ledge used a cast-iron and concrete base with a brick superstructure. Four light stations (including a pair of range lights) were established along the southern end of the Kennebec River in 1898. Reminiscent of several of the early nineteenth-century lighthouses, the new towers were octagonal wooden frame structures sheathed in wood shingles. Most other lighthouses built in this period repeated basic design forms used successfully in the past, and at Rockland Breakwater (1902) and The Cuckolds (1907) they were integrated into fog signal stations.

The last beacon to be erected in Maine was the Whitlock's Mill Light Station in 1910, ending more than a century of design and construction of lighthouses by masons, timber framers, architects, and engineers who diligently practiced their craft for the sake of greater safety at sea. Except for the earliest wooden structures, a remarkable number of the towers they built have survived. It is a legacy of lighthouse design that is among the richest in the United States.

This group of photographs illustrates the stylistic diversity and the often decorative nature of Maine's lighthouse stairs. Of particular note are the cantilevered granite steps at Wood Island (opposite page, top center) and the filigree-like cast-iron stairs at Baker Island (this page).

1

All Alone and Ever Ready

The Lives and Legends of the Keepers

Timothy Harrison

CHRISTMAS-EVE IN A LIGHT-HOUSE.—[SEE PAGE 1007.]

2

Since the earliest days of lighthouses, people have romanticized the life of the lighthouse keeper. Some have longed for the solitude of being away from the rest of the world at a light station on a quaint island or rocky ledge; others have dreamed of raising their families at some remote, yet beautiful, outpost; still others have wished for the thrill of being exposed to all the violent elements that nature could throw at them.

But life at many of those lighthouses was, in all reality, quite different from what most dreamed about. Long hours of physically arduous work alternated with periods of loneliness and boredom. Regardless of the location of their light stations, many of the keepers experienced unbelievable hardships while they served faithfully every day, often at great risk to themselves and their families.

Opposite page: Stevan Dohanos. *Saturday Evening Post.* June 26, 1954. Illustration © SEPS licensed by Curtis Licensing, Indianapolis, Indiana. All rights reserved.

3

Keeper Charles L. Knight can be seen above with Shep, the lighthouse dog, who was always ready to romp with the children of other keepers during Sunday visits. At right, Knight stands in front of Hendrick's Head Light, the third station he tended, after Squirrel Point (fig. 5) and Goose Rocks (fig. 4).

Keeper Charles L. Knight, who was stationed at a number of Maine lighthouses, recalled his first land-based assignment on the Kennebec River at Squirrel Point Light: "It was spring and the warm sunny days had begun. I thought every day was rosy. But I had no idea what an isolated section I was going into or the hardships I would have to put up with." After an amazing number of harrowing experiences rowing his children across the river back and forth to school, Knight asked for a transfer. He was sent to Goose Rocks Light, a round tower surrounded by water near the eastern entrance to the Fox Islands Thoroughfare, where his family was not allowed to live, but he was pleased with the assignment because his family could live ashore in a comfortable house, and he was allowed eight days off each month to visit them.

After twenty-eight years of service, Knight was finally transferred to Hendrick's Head Light in Boothbay Harbor, which he considered one of the best light stations because it included a house where he could be together with his family. But, even here, at a lighthouse on the mainland, he had to help rescue wreck victims, and he was on duty when a woman committed suicide in the waters off the lighthouse, an event that cast gloom over the family for a number of months.

4

Goose Rocks Light, Maine.

5

6

7

Hendricks Head Light, Maine.

The keepers were a close-knit group, corresponding by mail and visiting one another for special occasions when the weather permitted. Intermarriage between keeper families was common, and many children followed in their fathers' footsteps by becoming keepers themselves. One family, the Strouts, had a combined total of nearly 130 years of service, with over a hundred years just at Portland Head Light.

LIBBY ISLAND

12

13

14

16

15

17

Because of inclement weather, especially at remote lighthouses, the only gifts and special amenities that the keepers and their families might receive for Christmas came from the "Flying Santa," a program that was started in 1929 by the pilot, Captain William Wincapaw. One of his successors was historian and author Edward Rowe Snow, who is shown at right with his wife and daughter. The tradition is still carried on to this day by The Friends of the Flying Santa at lighthouses where Coast Guard personnel live and at other Coast Guard stations. But Santa no longer drops the presents from the air because he now lands by helicopter or boat and hand delivers the presents. (Figs. 18, 19)

FLYING
SANTA

21

22

23

NEMO.

Chang, pet dog of the Portland Head Light keeper Robert Thayer Sterling (both seen at left), was well known to the hundreds of people who visited the lighthouse. As well as being family pets, dogs at lighthouses gained worldwide fame by saving lives. Many of them have been immortalized in magazines, books, and memorials.

Many keepers kept animals, some as pets and others, like cows and chickens, to provide fresh milk and eggs for their families. Shep, the Knight family dog, was already something of a celebrity by the time he came to live at the lighthouse. As a young pup, he had been taken up for a flight by Charles Lindbergh during one of the aviator's many visits to Maine. But Shep's true fame was due to his keen sense of hearing. One night he started barking wildly, alerting Knight, who instinctively sounded the alarm that a boat in the harbor was in trouble, even though no vessel could be seen by the human eye. A young couple had lost their oars and were being swept out to sea. Thanks to Shep, they were rescued, and eventually the dog was awarded a bronze medal.

In the early 1900s at Heron Neck Light on Green's Island, two miles from Vinalhaven, keeper Levi Free-man's dog Nemo was renowned for his "fog-bark" which warned vessels away from hidden ledges. Every time the dog heard the sound of a boat's horn, he returned it with a bark, thus saving many vessels and lives. When the dog became too old to continue his duties, a new dog, Rover, was trained to take Nemo's place.

In the 1930s, Spot, the pet springer spaniel of keeper Gus Hamor at Owl's Head Light at the entrance to Rock-land Harbor, was known for pulling the rope that rang the fog bell every time he saw a vessel pass by. One day during a blinding snowstorm, the fog bell became frozen, causing Spot to begin barking frantically. Hearing the barking, the captain of a passing mailboat changed course and saved the vessel from smashing on the rocks. Today, a memorial stone at the lighthouse marks the ground where Spot is buried.

At those lighthouses where families were allowed to live, whether on the mainland or on an island, every member was trained to help with all aspects of maintaining the station, including how to keep the light burning. So it was not unusual when sixteen-year-old Abbie Burgess was left in charge of the twin towers at Matinicus Rock Light when her father, Samuel Burgess, went to the mainland, eighteen miles away, to get supplies in January 1856. Fierce weather kept him from returning for four weeks, but having been born on the island, Abbie knew everything she needed to do in his absence. During the lengthy storm, as waves swept over the island and flooded the keeper's house, Abbie, her sick mother, and her three sisters were forced to take refuge in one of the towers. Nevertheless, Abbie risked her life every day, wading through knee-deep water, which could have washed her out to sea, to keep the lights burning in the twin towers. The family would have run out of food had it not been for the eggs from Abbie's pet chickens, which she had rescued before their coop was swept away. Word of Abbie's bravery soon spread, and many tales of her dedication to duty appeared in newspapers and magazines around the world, causing her to become known as "Maine's lighthouse heroine."

When Abbie's father was replaced by John Grant as the lighthouse keeper at Matinicus Rock Light, Abbie agreed to remain at the lighthouse to help the new keeper's family familiarize themselves with the station. Soon, she fell in love with Isaac Grant (at right), John's son and the assistant keeper. The couple married and continued to live at Matinicus Rock, where they had four children, before being transferred to the light station on Whitehead Island. They served there until 1890 when they were forced to retire because of Abbie's declining health. Until then, Abbie had lived on an island lighthouse for her entire life. Shortly before her death in 1892, Abbie wrote that she hoped a lighthouse would be placed on her grave. But this did not happen until 1945 when historian and author Edward Rowe Snow put one there after learning about her wish. The metal lighthouse remains on Abbie's grave to this day.

In an 1891 letter, Abbie Burgess Grant wrote, "I wonder if the care of the lighthouse will follow my soul after it has left this worn-out body. If I ever have a gravestone, I would like it in the form of a lighthouse or beacon." Over fifty years after her death that wish finally came true.

28

29

30

Eighteen people from the wreck of the *Annie C. Maguire* were rescued by the family of Portland Head Light keeper Joshua Strout. His son Joseph recalled, "We sure had a full house. I never saw such a hungry tribe in all my life. We offered them hot coffee and fed them everything we had cooked. Lucky for those men, they came on a holiday and we had extra food cooked. Once they got that chicken pie into them, the whole gang wanted to stay."

Over the years, many keepers were awarded medals and commendations for their amazing rescues. One was Civil War hero Marcus Hanna, keeper at Two Lights in Cape Elizabeth, who saved two crewmen from the wreck of the schooner *Australia*. Charles Dobbins, keeper at Moose Peak Light from 1887 to 1905, was credited with saving the crew of the schooner *Ashton*. Joshua Strout, keeper at Portland Head Light, led the rescue that saved the crew of the schooner *Annie C. Maguire* when it struck on the rocks right next to the lighthouse on Christmas Eve in 1886. It became one of the most famous lighthouse shipwrecks in American history, thanks in part to the memorial placed on the rocky outcropping at the lighthouse by John A. Strout, who became the third generation of the Strout family to serve as a keeper there. With repainted lettering, the memorial to the ship survives as a reminder of the heroic rescue of everyone on board.

31

32

FRANK COFFIN

33

34

35

36

37

The government introduced standard uniform regulations in the late 1800s, but some variations were allowed. The keepers were required to wear the uniform whenever guests were present. In later years the brass buttons on their jackets featured a lighthouse. For the summer months a white uniform with white hat was allowed, but the white uniform was more popular in warmer climates and rarely used in Maine.

In 1917, while watching from shore, Rita Ingalls lost sight of her father, Petit Manan Light keeper Eugene Ingalls, as he was attempting to reach the mainland in a storm. Eugene's brother, Herman (above left), who was captain of the lighthouse tender *Zizania*, led the search and recovery efforts. In spite of this tragedy, Rita (on her mother's lap in the photograph above) grew up to love lighthouses, spending many summers with her grandfather, Herbert Robinson, who served as a keeper at a number of Maine lights.

41

42

Egg Rock Light, Frenchman Bay,

Wesley Dalzell was all dressed up on his last day at Egg Rock Light. He was too young to fully understand that he had to leave his lighthouse home after his father, keeper Clinton "Buster" Dalzell, had drowned while trying to reach the mainland.

43

Keepers faced danger often. In the early 1900s, veteran keeper James Hall was killed in a rock-blasting accident at Grindel Point Light, and in 1935, keeper Clinton "Buster" Dalzell mysteriously disappeared while rowing to the mainland from Egg Rock Light to do an errand. After his body was found, his pregnant widow and two small children had to leave the island and struggled to make a living.

Tragedy struck Petit Manan Light on December 29, 1916, when keeper Eugene Ingalls launched the station's powerboat to meet his wife, Inez, who was visiting her parents, Herbert and Mary Robinson, keepers at Moose Peak Light where Ingalls had previously served. Shortly after Ingalls left Petit Manan, a gale came up and his boat disappeared in the waves while his young daughter, Rita, watched from the lighthouse. His brother, Captain Herman Ingalls, captain of the lighthouse tender *Zizania*, spent several days searching for Eugene's body without success.

Keepers were proud of their unwavering dedication to duty, which they carried out without hesitation. In a bitter cold rain and sleet storm in March 1935, veteran keeper Alonzo Morong, who came from the well-known family of keepers, chose to spend the night in the unheated tower at Fort Popham Light on the Kennebec River. He had become drenched to the bone getting to the lighthouse where the winds and rain kept blackening the lens in the antiquated mantle lantern. Realizing that the lives of those on board the vessels on the river depended on the light, he stayed all night to keep the light shining brightly. By morning he had developed a bad chest cold that developed into pneumonia, and he died a few days later.

44

45

46

Although the lifeboat invented in the early 1900s by the Lubec Channel Light keeper Loring W. Myers (above) was considered a brilliant innovation, the big steamship companies opted for cheaper and less expensive lifeboats. Myers and others often said that if the R. M. S. *Titanic* had been outfitted with his lifeboats, more lives would have been saved.

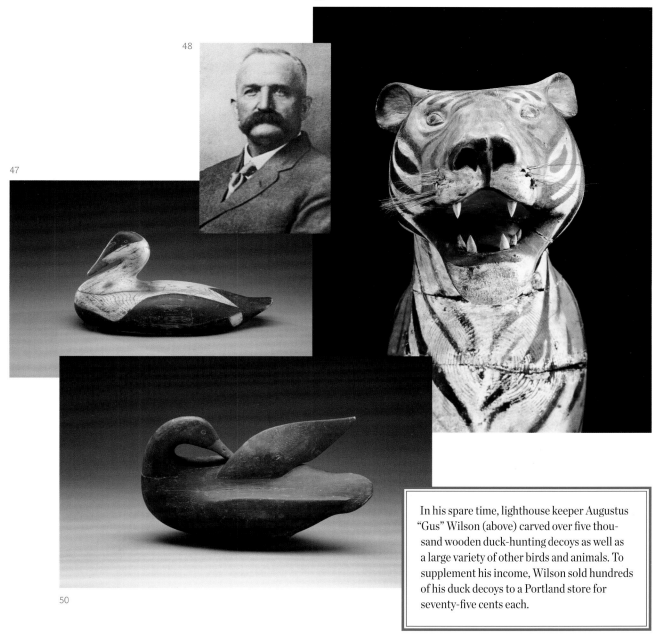

In his spare time, lighthouse keeper Augustus "Gus" Wilson (above) carved over five thousand wooden duck-hunting decoys as well as a large variety of other birds and animals. To supplement his income, Wilson sold hundreds of his duck decoys to a Portland store for seventy-five cents each.

Morong's brother, Frederick, Jr., became one the most famous figures in Maine's lighthouse history by writing a poem. Although not a keeper, he was the First District Machinist and later became the Lighthouse Inspector. He would often hear the keepers complain of polishing all the brass at lighthouses. Just for fun and for their enjoyment, one day while at Little River Light, he sat down and wrote the poem, "It's Brasswork."[1] Soon after the poem aired on a Boston radio station, it became so popular that it was known by keepers all over the nation and was posted at many lighthouses.

With time on their hands, many keepers came up with ingenious ways to make life easier or ways to supplement their income. In the 1930s, while stationed at St. Croix Island Light, keeper Elson Small built a windmill to generate power, which may have been the first use of green technology at an American lighthouse. Loring Myers, who served as keeper of the Lubec Channel Light for thirty-three years, invented a lifeboat that many sea captains hailed as revolutionary. Spring Point Ledge Light keeper Gus Wilson, who served there from 1917 to 1934, carved more than five thousand wooden bird decoys which he sold through a local store. Many believed that his were the best hand-carved decoys in America, and in 2005, one of his decoys sold at auction for nearly two hundred thousand dollars.

51

52

53

· LIFE ·

The Lighthouse Keeper

Voice (over the radio): Wondering where you are—and how you are—
and if you are—all alone—too. . . .

54

55

A JIG IN THE KEEPER'S PARLOR.

ENGRAVED BY PETER AITKEN.

TAXI

To make their lives easier as well as rewarding, the lighthouse keepers and their families had to be ingenious and imaginative in all of their daily activities. At St. Croix River Light, an island light station near Calais, keeper Elson Small barged a cow to the island for fresh milk as well as a truck so he would not have to carry supplies by hand from the boathouse to the keeper's house. Although there were no other families living on the island, he humorously dubbed his old truck the "Taxi," saying, "You won't find one of these on the streets of Times Square."

Seguin Light, Seguin Island, Me.

By the Sea

piano solo by
berenice benson bentley

Summy-Birchard Company
Evanston, Illinois

Whether it is folklore or fact, legend tells of
the lighthouse keeper at Seguin Light who
was driven to insanity by his wife's constant
playing of the same piano tune over and over
again. The outcome was deadly.

Not surprisingly, strange and bizarre legends have developed about many of Maine's lighthouses. At Boon Island Light off the coast of York, a nineteenth-century keeper settled with his new wife on the isolated rocky outcropping for what he thought would be a blessed life of isolation and love beneath the tallest lighthouse in Maine. During a violent storm, the keeper became ill and died. Although distraught, his wife managed to keep the light burning for three days, but after calm weather returned, she allowed the light to go out. When locals went to the island to find out what was wrong, they discovered her walking aimlessly on the rocks, having gone insane; she died a few weeks afterward. Later keepers reported seeing her ghost walking on the island's rocky edges, and one keeper's dog supposedly went mad as it followed her spirit around the tiny island, barking endlessly.

At Seguin Light, Maine's highest light above sea level, a young keeper brought a piano out to the lighthouse to help his young wife occupy her lonely hours. She played only one tune over and over again. Legend has it that the keeper bought new sheet music for his wife to learn, but she refused to do so. Finally the keeper snapped, took an ax to the piano and smashed it. In the ensuing argument, he axed his wife to death and then took his own life (although surely not with the ax). From time to time, and in all weather, many people who visit and fish the waters off Seguin claim that if you listen closely, you can still hear the music from the piano as the same song is played again and again.

In July 1939, the United States Lighthouse Service was dissolved and its duties taken over by the United States Coast Guard. The keepers could choose to stay on

July 28, 1923

The Literary Digest

(Title Reg. U.S.Pat.Off.)

THE LIGHTHOUSE-KEEPER'S DAUGHTER—By Norman Rockwell

New York FUNK & WAGNALLS COMPANY *London*

PUBLIC OPINION *New York* combined with *The* LITERARY DIGEST

Vol. 78, No. 4.   Whole No. 1736   July 28, 1923

Perhaps, as he stood gazing out to sea, Robert Thayer Sterling, the last civilian keeper of Portland Head Light, was recalling how he was able to live and record the last chapter of the United States Lighthouse Service in Maine and wondering what the future would hold for light stations under Coast Guard management.

as civilian keepers or join the Coast Guard. Most chose to stay as civilians until they retired and were replaced by Coast Guard keepers. Although a few lighthouses continued as family stations, automation changed lighthouse life forever. Gradually, keepers were removed and machines took over. The last light to be automated was Goat Island in 1990. Interestingly, it was still a family station when Brad and Lisa Culp, along with their two children, closed up the lighthouse, ending manned lighthouse-keeping in Maine forever.

Fortunately, some keepers like Robert Thayer Sterling, the last head keeper of the United States Lighthouse Service to serve at Portland Head Light, and others, such as Connie Scovill Small, wife of lighthouse keeper Elson Small, saved much of the history through their writings and photographs. Connie Small, who be-

came known as the "First Lady of Light" after publishing her memoirs in the book *The Lighthouse Keeper's Wife* at age eighty-five, gave over six hundred lectures during the course of her life, the last one being just a few days prior to her death in 2005 at age 103. The people who lived the lighthouse life all stressed that documenting the memories and preserving the photographs of their experiences were just as important as saving the actual structures themselves. Through their own efforts, they kept a record for future generations of a unique way of life at Maine's lighthouses that endured for over two hundred years until the automation of the lights put an end to it.

THE BOY WITH THE
U.S. LIFE SAVERS

FRANCIS ROLT-WHEELER

Children, Lighthouses, and Lifeboats

Stories of Danger and Rescue at Sea

Richard Cheek

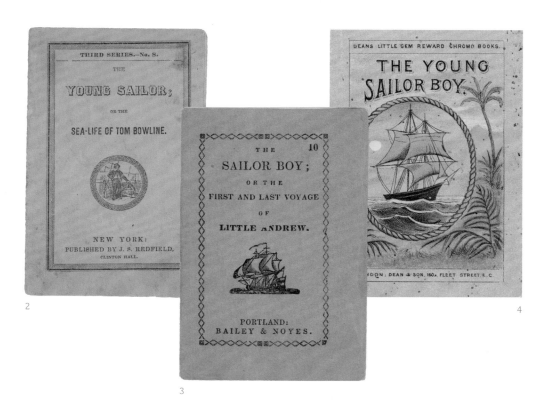

Until the middle of the nineteenth century, when light stations began to be systematically constructed all along America's coastlines rather than only in the most hazardous locations, lighthouses and the lifesaving equipment associated with them were a rarity in children's experience. With limited means of travel available, only those young people who happened to live near an existing beacon got to see one, and few lighthouses were ever mentioned or illustrated in the literature available to them.

That all began to change as lighthouses sprang up in noticeable numbers along the shore, especially in Maine, where thirty-seven new light stations were constructed or enlarged between 1820 and 1860. As passenger steamers began to regularly ply up and down the East Coast and as the railroad network expanded, children had a better chance to view lighthouses for themselves, but they also began to encounter them more frequently in the books and pamphlets they were given to read about the dangers of life at sea.

At first, lighthouses began to appear in existing forms of children's literature, such as ABCs, annuals, chapbooks, and primers. Most chapbooks—the cheap, small pamphlets that were popular in the eighteenth and early nineteenth centuries—were too early to feature lighthouses in the short stories or anecdotes they related, but they frequently dealt with the hardships and dangers of seafaring. Going to sea was seen by many boys as an exciting way to escape from home and church, so in order to discourage these potential runaways, many chapbooks that depicted life at sea, and the larger, hardbound storybooks that succeeded them, were admonitory in

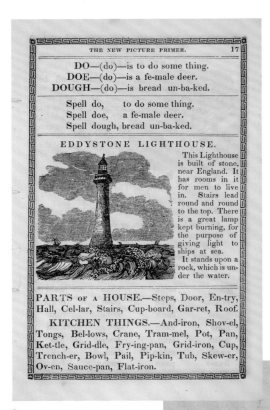

5

6

THE EDDYSTONE LIGHTHOUSE.

When lighthouses first appeared in children's literature, they were almost all modeled on the Eddystone Light off Plymouth, England, the world's most famous beacon.

7

tone, warning children against the moral and physical hazards of being a sailor and suggesting that if they were to become involved in a shipwreck, they would only be saved if they believed in God and had been obedient and thoughtful of others. In many examples, the intention of such publications was to literally frighten children into being devout and staying at home.

When lighthouses finally became part of the narrative, they were depicted by authors as warning signals, alerting sailors to the most treacherous points along the coast, or as devotional devices created by God to rescue mankind. The light of faith was shown shining forth from the towers to guide those who had strayed back to God, to keep them from being lost at sea in both the physical and spiritual sense. There were also great virtues to be observed and emulated in the monastic existence led by lightkeepers and their families, as demonstrated by *The Lighthouse* (c. 1850) published in England by the Society for Promoting Christian Knowledge (SPCK). The book traces the life of a keeper, his wife, and his children over the course of a generation, idealizing them as the model Christian family, faithful, patient, and persevering, but most importantly, willing to sacrifice themselves to save others. Children were also urged to be like a lighthouse themselves in *The Child's Companion and Juvenile Instructor* (1885): "First and foremost the love of God is our guiding light, but next to that, we can most help others by keeping a bright happy face . . . by being light-hearted and trustful, as dear children."

LIGHT-HOUSES.

Are lit up from sunset till sunrise. Some of them can be seen twenty miles off. They show sailors where the rocks are, and how to sail into harbor. Has God shown us how to get safe into heaven? Yes; and there is only one way, and unless we take Christ for our Pilot, we shall be lost.

To keep them from running away to sea, boys were warned of the dangers of shipwreck and the likelihood of drowning if they did not believe in God.

PERILS
OF THE
OCEAN,
OR
DISASTERS
OF THE
SEAS.
Embellished with twenty-two Engravings.

NEW-YORK:
MURPHY, Publisher,
384 Pearl-st.

The Sailor Boy.
Though the strained mast should quiver as a reed,
ring strew the gale,
N.

SHIPWRECKS
AND
DISASTERS AT SEA,
OR
HISTORICAL NARRATIVES
OF THE
MOST NOTED CALAMITIES, AND PROVIDENTIAL DELIVERANCES FROM
FIRE AND FAMINE, ON THE OCEAN.

Ye lost companions of distress, adieu!
Your toils and pains, and dangers are no more,
The tempest now shall howl unheard by you,
While ocean smiles in vain the trembling shore.
FALCONER

With a Sketch of the Various Expedients for Preserving the
LIVES OF MARINERS
BY THE AID OF
Life Boats, Life Preservers, &c.

COMPILED BY CHARLES ELLMS.

PHILADELPHIA:
JESPER HARDING
1846.

Older boys were thrilled to read stories of disasters at sea, especially if they were narrated by an old salt or accompanied by sensational illustrations.

Young children may have been frightened by tales that threatened them with drowning if they did not believe in God, but as they got older, they learned how to concentrate on the exciting parts and skip the moralizing sections. They were more partial to collections of shipwreck stories that had all of the thrills and none of the preaching, such as *The Boy's Book of Shipwrecks and Ocean Stories, Illustrating the Dangers and Hardships Incidental to a Nautical Life* (1851), with its many crude but graphic illustrations of terrible maritime disasters. They were also fond of story collections that had a friendlier narrator than the parson in his pulpit, such as tales of maritime derring-do that were told by an amiable old salt or retired captain. This, of course, was a printed version of the age-old method of passing on legends and myths from generation to generation, with a grizzled veteran speaking to an audience of spellbound children. One of the advantages of this approach was that the story was being told in the first person by the man who had experienced the events he was relating, and if his adventures began at an early age, it made it even easier for his young readers to identify with him.

One of the oldest and best loved books of this sort was *The Life, and Strange Surprizing Adventures of Robinson Crusoe; of York, Mariner* by Daniel Defoe, first published in England for adults in 1719 but widely available for children in abbreviated form with a shortened title and numerous illustrations from the late eighteenth century on. Here was the firsthand account of a man who leaves home without permission at age nineteen, takes ship to earn his fortune, and becomes the sole survivor of a wreck that deposits him on a desolate island in the middle of nowhere. All alone, he is forced to fend for himself until he is found and returned to England twenty-eight years later. No youth fretting under parental or Sunday school control could have asked for a better diversion, especially when it was so easy to skip over Robinson's prayerful interludes.

The enduring success of *Robinson Crusoe* with both juveniles and the very young spawned numerous imitations. Castaway books, along with land-based tales of orphans, became extremely popular throughout the nineteenth century as a vehicle for portraying the painful but ultimately fulfilling transition from childhood to adulthood. Typically, children and juveniles (boys much more often than girls) are cast adrift or left alone after a shipwreck in an isolated location devoid of any vestiges of a civilized society and are forced to look out for themselves. Only when the boys prove they can survive on their own, gaining maturity and demonstrating true independence, are they allowed to be rescued and to return home, completing their voyage of life.

The moral tale tradition, which emphasized the chief character's steadfast belief in God more than the events that tested his faith, was beginning to fade from children's literature, especially from stories intended for juveniles, largely due to the development of a new genre, loosely called the boys' adventure novel. Most of the later castaway books, and the first thrillers to feature lighthouses and lifeboats, fall into this category. The first successful historical adventure books had been written earlier in the century for adults, James Fenimore Cooper's Leatherstocking Tales (1823–1841) in America and Sir Walter Scott's Waverley novels (1814–1831) in Scotland, but both series had proved to be popular with young readers as well. Other British authors noticed this trend, and several of them decided to specialize in writing for teenage boys. Frederick Marryat (1792–1848) was first, followed by R. M. Ballantyne (1825–1894), W. H. G. Kingston (1814–1880), and G. A. Henty (1832–1902).

14

15

16

Based on the success of Daniel Defoe's *Robinson Crusoe*, tales of children or teenagers cast adrift or left alone after a shipwreck to fend for themselves in an isolated or uncivilized location became very popular with youthful readers of all ages from the beginning of the nineteenth century onward.

THE CASTAWAY SERIES

The Wonder Island Boy

THE CASTAWAYS OF DISAPPOINTMENT ISLAND

SCOTT-INMAN

THE LIAN FAMILY ROBINSON

LEE AND CAREY

ADRIFT IN A BOAT AND WASHED ASHORE

THE CASTAWAYS

James Oti

WRECKED ON A REEF

TWENTY MONTHS AMONG THE AUCKLAND ISLES

MASTERMAN READY

BY CAPTAIN MARRYA

Sixty Original Illustrations

THE CASTAWAYS

AN OCEAN ROMANCE

BY HARRY COLLINGWOOD

THE RIVAL CRUSOES

W. H. G. KINGSTON

Of these writers, Ballantyne was chiefly responsible for refining the elements that would typify boys' adventure novels from the 1860s until the end of the First World War: young boys are always the heroes; they are placed in exotic and dangerous locations where they become engaged in nonstop action against overwhelming odds that includes plenty of bloodletting, near-death experiences, and hairbreadth escapes; through grit, courage, get-up-and-go, and independent thinking, they always triumph in the end, rescuing others along the way and foregoing any love interest until their adventures are over.

Like his other British colleagues, Ballantyne was aware of the influence his books had on juveniles and was determined that his novels should serve the purposes of the Empire. But he was also aware that the nation needed to be served at home as well, so to that end he initiated a series of locally oriented adventure novels that placed his youthful heroes in crucial, contemporary professions that were inherently dangerous and required the same guts and determination to survive life-threatening situations in the course of doing one's duty. Significantly, the first two books to appear in this series were *The Lifeboat, A Tale of Our Coast Heroes* (1864) and *The Lighthouse* (1865). Ballantyne began with lifesaving and lightkeeping because these activities focused on preventing the loss of life at sea and were therefore vital to a maritime nation dependent upon its merchant and naval fleets for survival.

Appearing in the United States in pirated as well as authorized editions, Ballantyne's books and those of his fellow British adventure writers were almost as popular with American boys as they were with the loyal sons of the Crown. It was easy for young Americans to ignore the imperialistic implications (if they noticed them at all) for the sake of the thrilling events that flowed from one end of each of these books to the other. *The Lighthouse* is a typical example. Ballantyne manages to interweave an account of the erection of the Bell Rock Lighthouse from 1807 to 1811 on a dangerous tide-washed shoal near the mouth of the Firth of Forth with the romantic story of Ruby Brand, a strapping young Scotsman who joins the construction crew for the lighthouse in order to hide from Royal Navy press gangs while courting a golden-haired maiden named Minnie, an orphan who had been adopted by his mother. Thus the drama is set: will Ruby survive the series of accidents and storms that complicate the building of the lighthouse and the wreck he experiences after being pressed into the Navy and captured by the French in order to marry his sweetheart? Of course he does. Ruby escapes from the French by jumping ship during a storm near Bell Rock and swims to the lighthouse that has been successfully completed during his absence. He spends two nights at the lighthouse (so that he and we can be given a thorough tour) before being reunited with his mother and Minnie, whom he quickly weds.

31

32

33

A popular author of boys' adventure novels, R. M. Ballantyne focused two of his books on the most essential means for saving life at sea, *The Lifeboat* (1864) and *The Lighthouse* (1865).

In a typically dramatic scene from *The Lighthouse*, Scotsman Ruby Brand escapes from the French by jumping ship and swimming toward the Bell Rock Light that he had previously helped to construct. (Figs. 34, 35)

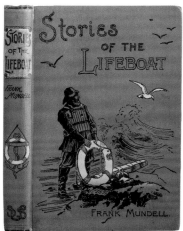

36

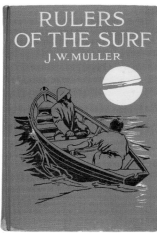

37

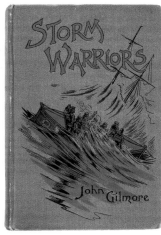

38

39

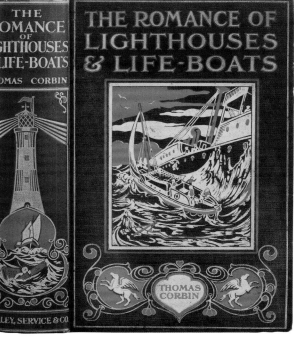

40

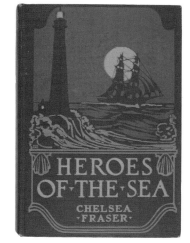

41

42

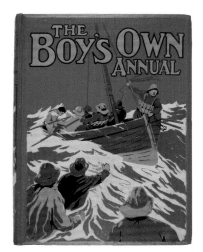

43

America had its own boys' adventure novelists, of course, such as Edward S. Ellis (1814–1916), Captain Mayne Reid (1818–1883), Kirk Munroe (1850–1930), and Edward Stratemeyer (1863–1930). One of the most prolific was Maine native James Otis Kaler (1848–1912), who wrote under the pseudonym of James Otis, presumably because it associated him with the Revolutionary hero of the same name. Following the same course as his moralizing Maine predecessor Elijah Kellogg (1813–1901) had steered, he wrote at least fifteen novels about teenagers at sea, fighting in two wars with the British, surviving shipwrecks, fishing for a living, or just cavorting about the islands off shore in the days when lighthouses either did not exist or were few and far between. Like so many of his American and English colleagues, Otis was serious about the factual and historical accuracy of his books because he was intent upon educating his readers as well as entertaining them. In fact, teaching history became such an imperative for him that he left his full-time job as a journalist (he only wrote novels on the side) to become the superintendent of the South Portland school system from 1898 until shortly before his death in 1912. Before he took that position, he had already begun to write semifictional accounts of what he considered to be the most important professions a boy could aspire to join: lifesaving, lighthouse-keeping, and firefighting. These were occupations crucial to the welfare of society as a whole, and he did everything he could to persuade young men to sign up by writing three service novels, *The Life Savers* (1896), *The Light Keepers* (1902), and *The Fire Fighters* (1904), the same three professions that Ballantyne had first promoted thirty or more years earlier. Neatly divided into chapters that highlighted the various aspects of these vital but dangerous trades, each book recounted a chronological series of adventures experienced by young male apprentices as they learned how to become competent lifesavers, lightkeepers, or firemen.

When it came to recruiting young men for the two services that prevented the loss of life at sea, nonfictional literature proved to be just as effective. During the second half of the nineteenth century, the oceans had become more and more crowded, leading to a great increase in the number and frequency of shipwrecks. These, in turn, required the erection of additional lighthouses and a major expansion in lifesaving capability. The number of men needed to keep the lights was limited, but sufficient manpower to crew the lifeboats proved to be harder to come by. As a consequence, there was a noticeable increase in the number of books published whose intention was to draw able-bodied young men to the rescue, beginning in the 1860s and reaching a crescendo in the early twentieth century.

Vivid accounts of rescues at sea, whether actual or imaginary, were crucial in recruiting young men for the U. S. Life-Saving Service from the 1860s through the 1920s.

THE WRECK OF THE 'TRIDENT.'—P 212.

44

SHIP ON THE ROCKS.

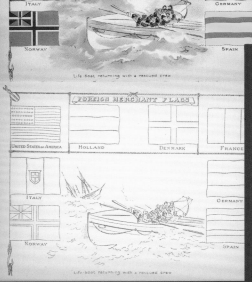

THE WRECK.

THE LICHTHOUSE.

THE RESCUE.

THE JOLLY TAR.

45

46

47

OFF TO THE WRECK.

Younger children learned about lighthouses and lifeboats through ABCs, coloring books, and picture books full of striking images.

Let ter   Lev el   Le ver

Lew is   Life boat   Light house

48

49

The brave exploits of three young women in the mid-nineteenth century—Grace Darling in Scotland, Ida Lewis in Rhode Island, and Abbie Burgess in Maine—spawned a succession of stories and novels about girls living in lighthouses and performing as heroically under storm and stress as men that continues to this day.

Although almost all of the books mentioned up to this point were written for boys, there has also been a strong tradition of lighthouse literature for girls stemming from the heroics of an English lightkeeper's fifteen-year-old daughter, Grace Darling. On the evening of March 25, 1837, when she saw that no one was available to save the passengers from a nearby wreck except her father, she immediately jumped into a dory to help row him to the rescue of as many people as they could jointly haul aboard. Almost immediately, the incident became internationally famous, inspiring numerous songs, poems, and prose tributes, and from then on, Grace Darling's name almost always appeared in any children's or juvenile book that celebrated heroic girls or women. Later in the century, when Ida Lewis played a similar role in pulling drowning victims to safety from wrecks off Newport, Rhode Island, and Abbie Burgess kept the lights burning at Matinicus Rock in Maine during the three weeks of storms in the winter of 1856 that had kept her father from returning, their brave exploits eventually spawned a succession of short stories and novels that have young girls living in lighthouses and performing traditionally male activities. That stream of books continues to this day, to the point that there are now more children's books in print that have girls interacting with lighthouses than there are featuring boys.

From a historical perspective, the initial cause for this shift in focus was purely circumstantial: in the absence of the keeper or any other male, Ida and Abbie were forced by conditions beyond human control to perform actions that were normally the province of men, and in so doing, they demonstrated the same strength of mind and character under severe physical stress as men were expected to show. The suggestion that girls might be just as capable of independent thinking and deliberate action as boys was not an idea that the late nineteenth century in general was ready to accept. Such exceptional behavior was often attributed to the direct intervention of God, as was the case with Little Mary in *The Lighthouse-Keeper's Daughter—A True Story* (1862) who was unable to reach

the lamps that needed to be lit after her father had been kidnapped by wreckers until she prayed and was then inspired by the Lord to place the large family Bible underneath a ladder to give herself the extra height she needed. This story proved to be so popular that it was repeated in Asa Bullard's *The Lighthouse* (1863) and in Rev. Barry L. Blake's *The Watchers on the Longships* (1876).

In most nineteenth-century literature related to the dangers of seafaring, women and children were portrayed as helpless victims when disaster occurred. In scenes depicting shipwrecks, for example, the most heartrending illustrations were always the ones showing a woman with a child in her arms about to be drowned unless a male hand could reach her in time.

"The Bible was placed on the chair, and over it the basin, upon which Mary climbed," &c.—*P.* 209.

The Mother felt the Child slipping, and a piercing shriek
escaped from her.'—P. 331.

" IT'S A CHILD, ALICK ! " HE SAID.   " PUT IT DOWN
BY YOU.

In most nineteenth-century literature dealing with
the dangers of seafaring, women were portrayed as
helpless victims when shipwrecks occurred who
could only be rescued by men. (Figs. 55–58)

Captain January

Laura E. Richards

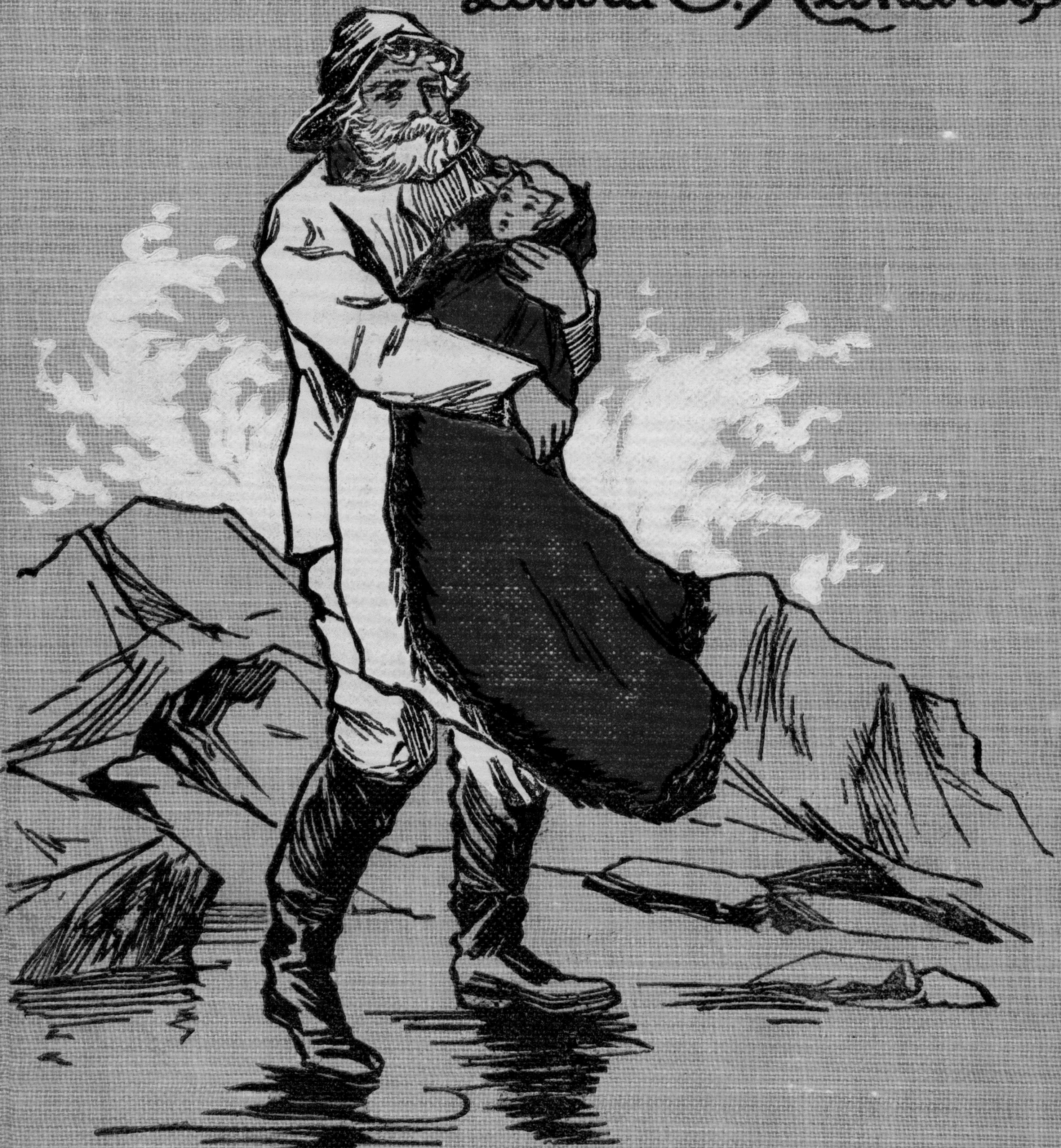

59

As a consequence, the few girls placed in fictional lighthouse stories during the nineteenth century were cherished and well-protected and only occasionally allowed to act like tomboys. By far the most notable example of this cosseted state of being occurred in *Captain January*, first published in 1890 by Laura E. Richards (1850–1943). The daughter of Samuel Gridley Howe and Julia Ward Howe, she lived much of her life in Maine and wrote approximately eighty children's books.

The book unfolds dramatically. Wrapped in a sail and tied to a spar, a little girl of unknown origin is washed up barely alive in the arms of her dead mother on an island with a lighthouse in Maine and is discovered and nursed back to health with great delight by the lonely old former sea captain who is now the light's keeper. He names her Star Bright and adopts her, and she becomes the light of his life and of all those who get to know her.

Ten years later, Star Bright's resemblance to her mother is noticed by a passenger on a steamer temporar-ily grounded nearby, who turns out to be her Aunt Isabel. When Isabel and her husband come to the lighthouse to reclaim the girl for her family, they relent when they see how much she loves her "Daddy Captain." They allow her to stay until the captain receives his final orders from the Lord and dies quietly in his favorite chair.

Instead of serving as the site for the orphan girl's painful passage to maturity, the isolated location of the lighthouse simply allows the captain to keep Star Bright all to himself. Smart, playful, vivacious, loving, and respectful, she is the ideal daughter he never expected to have. Gone are the tribulations that plagued the lives of other castaways who ended up on islands with predatory animals or hungry cannibals. Star Bright was assured of a happy, fulfilling life the moment she was rescued by the captain, and consequently her story warmed the hearts of many generations of Americans, in good times and bad, and led to the making of two movies, the first with Baby Peggy in 1924 and the second with Shirley Temple in 1936.

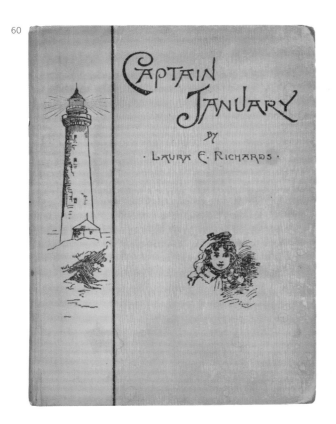

The most popular novel ever published about a girl growing up at a light station in Maine (or anywhere else in America) was Laura Richards's *Captain January* (1890). Once she was rescued from a shipwreck, Star Bright led a charmed life in both book and cinema, free of the dangers and the mental and physical challenges that would test the mettle of girls in lighthouse stories published after World War I.

64

65

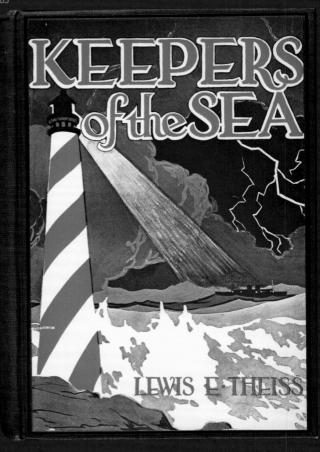

66

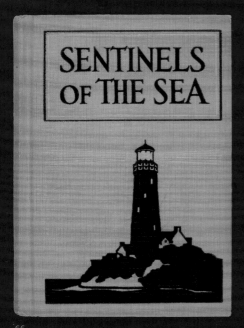

67

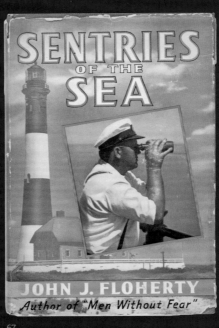

68

The first book to deliberately educate children about lighthouses was Mary Bradford Crowninshield's *All Among the Lighthouses* (1886). It was a travel novel set in a lighthouse tender as it visited the stations along Maine's coast. Histories that emphasized the technical and practical aspects of the lights began to be published in the 1920s.

In spite of its popularity, *Captain January* was one of the last books featuring girls in a lighthouse setting to treat them as charming but relatively helpless members of the weaker sex. In early twentieth-century books for both young children and juveniles, girls whose lives revolved around a lighthouse became progressively more "modern," tomboyish in some cases or more resourceful and independent-minded as they got older. After the First World War, those who were cast in the Grace Darling or Abbie Burgess role in a contemporary setting, such as fifteen-year-old Georgina in *Watty & Company* (1919), stepped in to remedy crisis situations in a matter-of-fact, "there was no other choice" manner, as if to suggest that any clear-thinking and reasonably courageous young person would act that way, whether male or female.

This more balanced approach toward youthful interaction with lighthouses is also reflected by the histories of the stations that began to appear in the 1920s and continued to be published through the 1970s. They were written for both boys and girls with more emphasis on the technical and practical aspects of the lights—their purpose, construction, engineering, and maintenance—than on the events that may have occurred around them. Some still suggested their role as guardians or protectors—*Sentinels of the Sea* (1926) or *Sentries of the Sea* (1942)—but they all tended to focus on the facts rather than the drama. One of these books is of particular note: Mary Ellen Chase's *The Story of Lighthouses* (1965). Chase (1887–1973) was born in Maine and served as a professor of English at Smith College for thirty years, writing many seafaring novels set in Maine and historical and biographical books related to the state. Although her book intended to be a general history, it features Matinicus Rock and Mount Desert Rock as two of the most remote and hardest to maintain lighthouses in America.

69

70

The days of frequent shipwrecks are now past, thanks not only to the completion of an overlapping network of coastal and island lighthouses, but also to the development of other navigational aids such as radio beams, radar, and GPS. Far fewer ships are now lost because of fog or storms, and those that do become imperiled in a gale are often out to sea, out of sight, where rescues are accomplished by the Coast Guard, using cutters, larger vessels, and helicopters. As a consequence, lifeboats are no longer needed, and the books that celebrated the heroic actions of their crews have disappeared.

The fact that lighthouses are now less necessary than they used to be is cause for celebration, but the automation of the beacons and the decommissioning of many of the stations has not led to a reduction in the amount of literature available to children that relates their lore and history. Because more lighthouses are now accessible to the public and are easier to reach by boat, car, train, or plane, more children are visiting them than ever before, spurred on by a rich array of lighthouse-related books varying from activity books and histories to dozens of picture books, mysteries, and ghost stories.

Not surprisingly, a large percentage of all lighthouse books available for children today feature Maine beacons. Thanks to Abbie Burgess's exploits, there are at least seven books that depict a girl from ten to sixteen years old bravely standing in to keep a Maine light burning while the keeper is absent or disabled, and of all the cats and dogs and other animals who are shown playing similar lifesaving roles in picture books, the majority display their valor at a Down East light station. Fortunately for future generations of young readers, this wonderful stream of literature will continue to flow from Maine's lighthouses, inspired by their history and perpetuating the ideal of brave, selfless action to save those in peril on the sea.

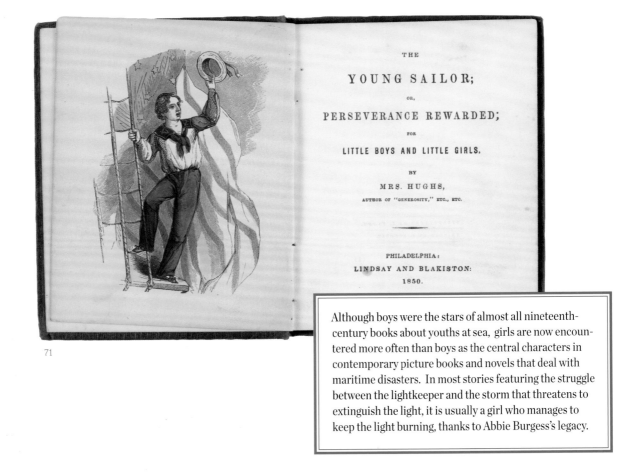

71

Although boys were the stars of almost all nineteenth-century books about youths at sea, girls are now encountered more often than boys as the central characters in contemporary picture books and novels that deal with maritime disasters. In most stories featuring the struggle between the lightkeeper and the storm that threatens to extinguish the light, it is usually a girl who manages to keep the light burning, thanks to Abbie Burgess's legacy.

The Lighthouse Keeper's Daughter
by Arielle North Olson

Illustrated by Elaine Wentworth

Abbie Against The Storm

THE
TRUE STORY OF
A YOUNG HEROINE
AND A
LIGHTHOUSE

Written by Marcia Vaughan
Illustrated by Bill Farnsworth

HISTORY'S KID
HEROES

THE STORMY
ADVENTURE OF
ABBIE BURGESS,
LIGHTHOUSE
KEEPER

BY PETER ROOP AND CONNIE ROOP
ADAPTED BY AMANDA DOERING TOURVILLE
ILLUSTRATED BY ZACHARY TROVER

1

LIBERTY
DEMOCRACY
U.S.
C R MILLER
DON'T LET THAT
LIGHT GO OUT
THINKAMERICAN INSTITUTE
THINKAMERICAN No. 60—COPYRIGHT, MCMXL, KELLY-READ & CO., ROCHESTER, N. Y.

Nation, Home, and Heaven

The Moral Significance of Lighthouses

Richard Cheek

2

Beyond their utility as seamarks to warn mariners away from rocks and reefs, lighthouses have come to be valued as important symbols of national identity, domestic well-being, and religious belief.

Seafaring countries have always had to build beacons along their coasts to protect their mercantile and military fleets from destruction during storms and foggy conditions, but they were also quick to realize the propaganda value of constructing the largest possible tower or of placing one in an especially difficult location. In the ancient world, the Egyptians built the Pharos of Alexandria to a much larger scale than was necessary for navigational purposes, and the Greeks erected the Colossus of Rhodes to intimidate those who passed beneath its giant legs as much as to guide them safely into harbor. In more modern times, the English so successfully publicized the engineering feats that enabled them to build a succession of four lighthouses from 1759 through 1882 on an incredibly dangerous reef off Plymouth that the Eddystone Lighthouse became the world's most famous beacon. Although the United States was a late entrant into this international competition, constructing its first lighthouse at Boston in 1787, it eventually built more lighthouses in a shorter amount of time than any other country, towers that came to be seen by its citizens as protecting political and religious freedom and projecting the light of democracy across the oceans to the rest of the world.

Greece and Rome knew the value of protecting their ships and projecting their power with lighthouses, but it was ancient Egypt that managed to build the tallest tower, the Pharos of Alexandria, destined to become one of the Seven Wonders of the World.

In more modern times, the Eddystone Lighthouse became the world's most famous beacon because of Great Britain's success in publicizing the engineering feats that enabled the country to erect a succession of four towers on a dangerous, wave-swept reef off Plymouth, England.

JANUARY 1937
25 CENTS

BEACON LIGHTS
OF
PATRIOTISM

CARRINGTON

SILVER, BURDETT & COMPANY

The *American*
LEGION
MONTHLY

10

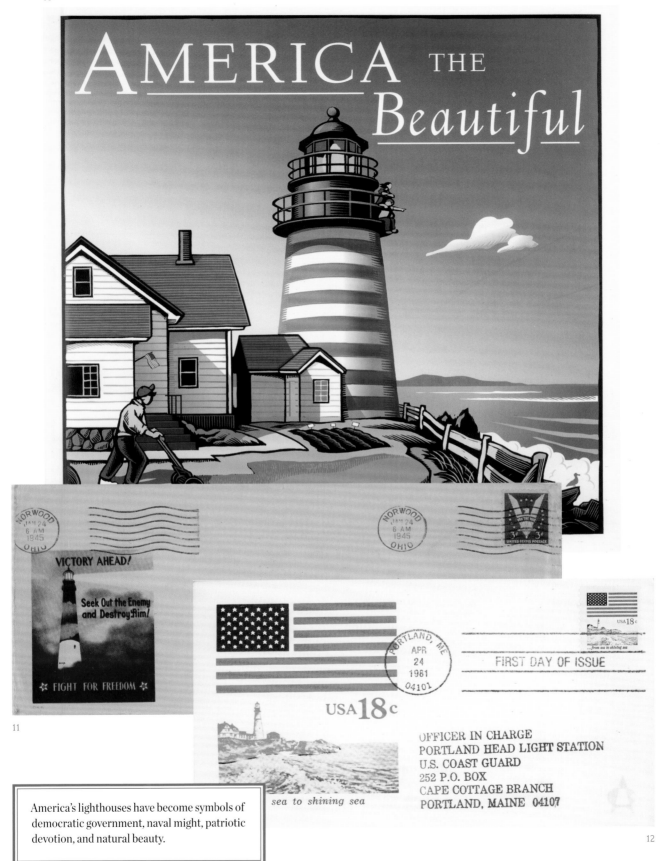

America's lighthouses have become symbols of democratic government, naval might, patriotic devotion, and natural beauty.

11

12

13

PATRIA

H. Scott.

Every maritime nation takes pride in its lighthouses as emblems of safety, security, and technical achievement, as demonstrated by this frontispiece from a book on the coast of France and four trade cards published in French for the Liebig Extract of Meat Company of London.

PHARES.
Phare de Rotesand.

Allemagne.

Appareil
d'éclairage dioptrique.

VÉRITABLE EXTRAIT DE VIANDE **LIEBIG.**

VOIR L'EXPLICATION AU VERSO.

Portugal.

PHARES.
Cap St. Vincent.

Sauvetage par des pilotes.

VÉRITABLE EXTRAIT DE VIANDE **LIEBIG.**

VOIR L'EXPLICATION AU VERSO.

PHARES.
Constantza.

Roumanie.

Pavillons à signaux.   Canon pour signaux

VÉRITABLE EXTRAIT DE VIANDE **LIEBIG.**

VOIR L'EXPLICATION AU VERSO.

Italie.

PHARES.
Phare de Messine.

Bateau piloté italien.

Faisant le point au moyen du sextant.

VÉRITABLE EXTRAIT DE VIANDE **LIEBIG.**

VOIR L'EXPLICATION AU VERSO.

18

19

20

My Hope is in the LORD;
My works I count but dust;
I build not there, but in His Word,
And in His goodness trust.

Up to His care myself I yield:
He is my Tower, my Rock, my Shield,
And in His help I tarry.

And though it linger till the night,
And round again to morn,
My heart shall ne'er mistrust Thy might,
Nor count itself forlorn.

Luther. Translated by C. Winkworth.

Belief in God gave shipwrecked sailors a chance for salvation, as represented by the statues of Hope holding her anchor of faith that can be seen standing above the graves of merchants, seamen, and their family members in many New England graveyards.

If great lighthouses represent the technical and maritime might of the nations that build them, then they can also be viewed as symbols of the power of God. From the fundamental Christian perspective, it is the light of faith that shines forth from the towers to guide men safely home on earth and to lead them to their final port in heaven. The Dark Ages that followed the collapse of the Roman Empire were given that name because heathen tribes snuffed out most cultural and intellectual activities, but the period was literally darker because all of the coastal beacons the Romans had erected in an empire-wide system had been extinguished. The first warning fires to be relit were in the steeples of churches and monasteries along the coast of medieval Europe, but as dim and inadequate as they were, they came to be associated with the rekindling of belief in the one and only God.

By the time the erection of lighthouses had been resumed on a regular basis by mercantile powers in the sixteenth century, it was generally believed that it was the guiding light of the Lord that illuminated the braziers and beacons and provided mankind with the only hope of surviving the vicissitudes of life on earth. Journeys at sea were equated with the voyage of life, and shipwrecks were viewed as a test of faith because only those who truly believed in God would be saved, in soul if not in body. Fate was unpredictable, so even the faithful might drown, but if a righteous life had been led up to that point, eternal salvation was assured.

This fear of an almighty God who controlled the seven seas with an unknowable will still predominated at the beginning of the nineteenth century, and sermons directed at American sailors often threatened them with annihilation if they were immoral in their behavior. A famous example was the "Address to Seamen" presented by the Rev. Edward Payson (1800–1893) to an overflow crowd at the Second Church in Portland on October 28, 1821. Warning his "shipmates" to steer clear of Drunkard's Rock and the Whirlpool of Bad Company, he urged them to adopt the Bible as their chart and to accept Christ as their pilot. As they passed through the Straights of Repentance and entered the Bay of Faith, they would encounter a high hill, called Mount Calvary.

On top of this hill stands a Light-House, in the form of a cross; which, by night, is completely illuminated from top to bottom, and by day, sends up a pillar of smoke, like

SAILORS' HYMN.

I was once far away from the Saviour,
  And as vile as a sinner could be;
I wondered if Christ, the Redeemer,
  Would save a poor sinner like me.

I wandered on in the darkness,
  Not a ray of light could I see,
And the thought fill'd my heart with sadness,
  There's no hope for a sinner like me.

But there in that dark lonely hour,
  A voice sweetly whispered to me,
Saying, "Christ the Redeemer hath power'
  To save a poor sinner like me.

I listened, and lo, 'was the Saviour,
  That was speaking so kindly to me;
I cried, "I'm the Chief of Sinners,"
  Thou canst save a poor sinner like me.

I then fully trusted in Jesus,
  And oh, what a joy came to me,
My heart was filled with His praises,
  For He saved a poor sinner like me.

And when life's journey is over,
  And I the dear Saviour shall see;
I'll praise Him forever and ever,
  For saving a sinner like me.

Please hand this to the Lady or Gentleman.
WILL CALL IN ONE OR TWO HOURS.
THIS COPY FOR SALE.

NO. 140.

AN

Address to Seamen,

DELIVERED BEFORE THE

PORTLAND MARINE BIBLE SOCIETY.

BY REV. EDWARD PAYSON, D. D

See pages 8, 9.

PUBLISHED BY THE

AMERICAN TRACT SOCIETY,

AND SOLD AT THEIR DEPOSITORY, NO. 144 NASSAU-STREET, NEAR
THE CITY-HALL, NEW-YORK; AND BY AGENTS OF THE
NCHES, AND AUXILIARIES, IN
AL CITIES AND TOWNS
UNITED STATES.   **H 2**

In the allegorical woodcut that accompanied the printed version of the Rev. Edward Payson's "Address to Seamen," the stormy Sea of Despair is depicted to the left of the Straits of Redemption that separate it from the peaceful Bay of Faith on the right.

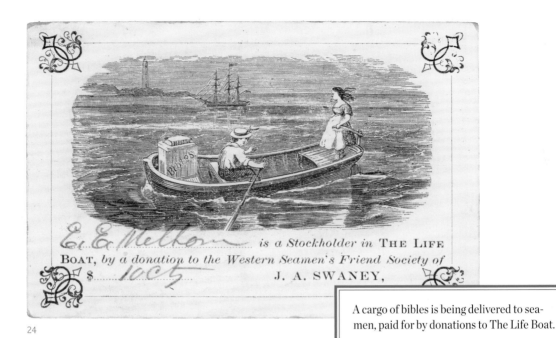

24

a white cloud. It stands so high, that, unless you deviate from the course laid down in your chart [the Bible], you will never lose sight of it in any succeeding part of your voyage. At the foot of this Light-House, you will find the Pilot I have so often mentioned, waiting for you. You must by all means receive Him on board; for without Him, neither your own exertions, nor all the charts and pilots in the world can preserve you from fatal shipwreck.

Although still in the "storm and shipwreck" mode of preaching that threatened damnation, Payson's sermon differed from its predecessors in two significant ways. First, he used nautical language that would be familiar to mariners, rather than traditional religious rhetoric. Second, he told the sailors that they were capable of saving their own souls. Although Payson was a Protestant who believed in original sin—that mankind was inherently sinful—he no longer shared the doctrinal view that God's grace and the remission of sin could only be achieved through the auspices of the clergy in a formally organized church. On the contrary, he believed that if a man could be persuaded to openly admit his sinfulness and accept the Bible as his guide and Christ as his savior, he could alter his own character and earn his way to heaven by himself.

Payson was in the forefront of a Christian fundamentalist revival, often called the Second Great Awakening, that began to take hold in the 1830s. Although Payson did have his own church, many fundamentalist minis-

ters became itinerant preachers who traveled all over New England, setting up tents and inviting everyone or anyone, rich or poor, famous or unknown, to come listen to the new promise: if you could take the Bible into your heart and come to truly believe in Jesus, you could gain a place in heaven by yourself.

Wayward seamen had long been a problem for established churches because whenever they were at sea, they were beyond spiritual control. Without membership in a church or the moral guidance of a minister, they were bound to behave badly. But the fundamentalists believed they could solve this dilemma by organizing churches specifically for seamen to attend when they were in port, such as the 1829 Mariner's Church in Portland (below), or by establishing bible societies, both of which sought to provide sailors with a free bible that they could take back on board ship with them.

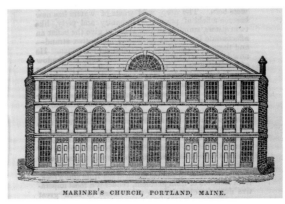

MARINER'S CHURCH, PORTLAND, MAINE.

25

RETURN, O wanderer,
to thy home,
Thy Father calls
for thee:
No longer now an
exile roam,
In sin and
misery.

J·F·

meaning:-

"In a dangerous position."

26

As the influence of the Second Great Awakening extended nationally, an increasing amount of literature began to be produced to encourage religious devotion and clean living at all levels of society, facilitated by steady advances in printing techniques and paralleling the great expansion of lighthouse construction from 1830 until the onset of the Civil War. Much of this writing, from poems and song lyrics to didactic stories and novels, revolved around sailors, fishermen, and the vicissitudes of life at sea and was produced with the hope of encouraging brave and godly behavior in the face of danger. Lighthouses were frequently featured in these tales, not just as the source of God's guiding light, but also as a symbol of the mariner's final destination at the end of his lifetime voyage, heaven itself. Beyond the metaphors, however, those who kept the lights were portrayed as models of Christian strength, patient, steadfast, and vigilant. Equally admirable were the men who risked their lives to save the victims of shipwrecks. Such heroism and self-sacrifice on the part of keepers and lifeboat crews were endlessly dramatized and extolled, not just in fictional works but in factual accounts published in sermons, books, magazines, and newspapers.

WHEN THE FOUNDATION GOES, THE LIGHT IS DOOMED

27

HE breeze blows fair, and the lovely shore
Glows with the crimson of sunset light,
The ocean waves, like a jewelled floor,
Up-bear the barque in her skimming flight.

BUT, Christian Mariner, not for thee
As yet are the toil and danger o'er;
For the quicksands that thou canst not see,
And the sharp-toothed rocks begird the shore.

MARK well the chart, watch unto prayer,
For danger lurks in the sunniest sea;
Of hidden peril do thou beware,
Lest the barque be wrecked eternally.

28

THE ETERNAL GOD IS THY REFUGE, AND UNDERNEATH ARE THE EVERLASTING ARMS.

ART CARD CO. ALAMEDA, CALIF. No. 37

★ BLESSING STAMP ★

Literature published to encourage religious devotion after 1850 frequently used the image of a lighthouse to represent the source of God's light, the church as an essential institution, or heaven as the final port of call.

The Lord is my light. Ps. 27:1

The human life voyage is thickly beset on every side with the reefs of temptation and the rocks of sin. God has put light houses along the coast.

"Ye are the light of the world."

"Let your light so shine before men that they may see your good works and glorify your Father which is in heaven." M.R.P.

29

The Lord is my light. 27:1

I will make darkness light before them. Isa. 42:16

God's precious promises! if we cherish them they shine out along life's pathway to light up many a dark spot. Beacon Lights! may they be such to you; and not the flashing but fixed,—that you may never lose sight of them for one moment. Capt. H.A.B.

30

The influence of such literature upon the seamen themselves is hard to gauge, especially since many sailors were unable to read. But fortunately for all mariners, the religious and charitable community in New England was as concerned with their physical welfare as it was with their spiritual condition. The onset of the Second Great Awakening had not only sparked a drive for moral self-improvement amongst all faiths, but it had also helped to impel an effort to reform the ills of American society in general. The reform movement spread in many directions, as temperance unions, abolition organizations, relief societies, and utopian communities began to be founded from the 1820s onward.

One of the problems that drew particular attention was the lack of any organized national lifesaving system to reduce the terrible attrition resulting from the increasing number of shipwrecks along the coasts and within the Great Lakes. Although the Massachusetts Humane Society had begun to build lifeboat stations along the state's coast in 1807, no other private groups followed suit until a New Jersey representative persuaded Congress to fund a small system in his state in 1848. After a series of well-publicized shipwrecks in 1850, the federal government finally began to get involved in building lifesaving stations, but it was not until 1878 that the United States Life-Saving Service was formally established under General Superintendent Sumner Increase Kimball, a Maine man from Lebanon who ran the Service successfully until it was absorbed by the Coast Guard in 1915.

A Thomas Nast cartoon satirizes the federal government's reluctance to fund lifesaving activities. After the U. S. Life-Saving Service was finally established in 1878, its heroic actions were well celebrated in books, magazines, and newspapers.

DEATH ON ECONOMY.

U. S. "I suppose I must spend a little on Life-saving Service, Life-boat Stations, Life-Boats, Surf-Boats, etc.; but it is too bad to be obliged to waste so much money."

31

THE UNITED STATES LIFE SAVING SERVICE.

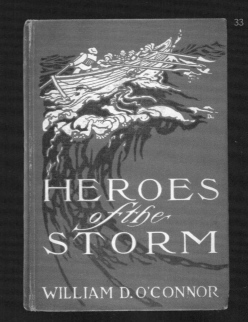

HEROES
of the
STORM

WILLIAM D. O'CONNOR

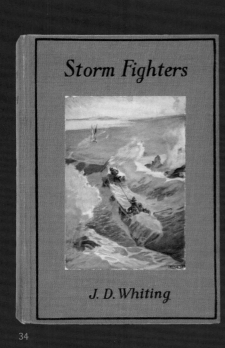

Storm Fighters

J. D. Whiting

PERILS OF THE COAST—THE LIFE-SAVING SERVICE.—Drawn by M. J. Burns.—[See Page 251.]

THE LIGHT THAT FAILS
—Harding in the Brooklyn *Eagle.*

36

37

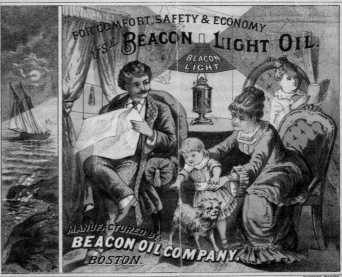

FOR COMFORT, SAFETY & ECONOMY
USE BEACON LIGHT OIL.

MANUFACTURED BY
BEACON OIL COMPANY.
BOSTON.

38

Home again, home again from a foreign shore;
And oh, it fills my soul with joy
To meet my friends once more.

And when he cometh home he calleth together
his friends and neighbors saying unto them, Rejoice with me.
Luke 15-6

A happy home was regarded as a mainstay of nineteenth-century society, an ideal that was often romanticized by images of returning sailors yearning for the first glimpse of the lighthouse that signaled their home port. But seamen on long voyages were beyond domestic influence, and many were unmarried with no home to return to.

HOME AGAIN

Home again, home again, home again

39

40

The Portland Marine Society was founded in 1807, but its activities were designed to benefit merchants and ship captains, not ordinary seamen. Any action on behalf of homeless or indigent sailors was left to the bethel chapels and the bible and temperance societies, few of which could afford to offer much care in Maine beyond the distribution of bibles and pamphlets.

The next challenge confronting both the federal government and the reform movement was how to care for seamen once they were back on shore, regardless of their manner of arrival. Those who were sick or disabled required medical attention, but all of them needed a place to stay.

Hoping to utilize the government health tax of twenty cents a month that customs officers had been collecting from sailors since 1798, charitable organizations and congressional politicians in Portland tried and failed numerous times in the first half of the nineteenth century to raise sufficient funds to build a seamen's hospital. Success was finally achieved in 1859 when the U. S. Marine Hospital opened on Martin's Point.

Providing shelter for sailors was an even harder task. A happy home was regarded as one of the mainstays of nineteenth-century society, an ideal that was frequently represented by the image of a lighthouse lantern, signaling the location of a safe harbor to each sailor and reminding him of the light in the window of his home where his family was waiting to welcome him. But the reality was that many mariners were unmarried and had no home to go to, so they became displaced citizens in a community that was often anxious to see them go back to sea. The presence of returned but homeless sailors could have undesirable social consequences, especially when they sought solace at taverns or brothels to fill the empty hours. Hence local relief agencies were privately established to provide such men with a temporary refuge and more wholesome sources of amusement, and in some cases, to offer old salts and disabled seamen a place to retire. One of the first to be organized was the American Seamen's Friend Society in 1828. Its constitution clearly stated its humanitarian purposes:

To improve the social and moral condition of seamen, by uniting the efforts of the wise and good in their behalf; by promoting in every port boarding houses of good character, savings banks, register offices, libraries, museums, reading rooms and schools; and also the ministrations of the gospel, and other religious blessings.

In spite of the religious community's attempts to focus attention on the victims of shipwrecks, advertisers could not resist taking advantage of the public's fascination with disasters to push their products, such as the spool of thread whose strength could save lives.

41, 42

One of the most moving expressions of this spirit of brotherly love was a temperance hymn written in 1888 by the Rev. Edwin S. Ufford, onetime minister of the Galilee Temple in Rockland. After witnessing a lifesaving demonstration, he returned home to compose both lyrics and music for "Throw Out the Lifeline," an appeal to action to save those in mortal or spiritual distress.

Throw out the lifeline to danger-fraught men
Sinking in anguish where you've never been;
Winds of temptation or billows of woe
Will soon throw them out where the dark waters flow.

Throw out the lifeline across the dark wave;
There is a brother whom someone should save;
Someone's brother! Oh, who then will dare
To throw out the lifeline, his peril to share?

No matter whether the sailor needed to be rescued from drink or the sea, the song became one of the most popular hymns of the late nineteenth century and is still sung in churches and at concerts today.

Fortunately, steady improvements in shoreline navigational aids, shipboard and satellite guidance systems, and shipbuilding during the twentieth century have made seafaring much less hazardous, so that the sailor's need for rescue, succor, and refuge because of wrecks along the coast has almost been eliminated. Modern health and social services are now readily available in every port. As a consequence, the lifesaving stations have shut down, the mariners' temples are gone, and most of the sailors' homes have closed, but the lighthouses remain, reminding Maine's citizens of their fine heritage of national, civic, and religious ideals.

BELDING BROS. & CO.'s LIFE SAVING SERVICE

"IT WILL BRING THEM SAFE TO SHORE"

In my distress
I called upon the
LORD,
and cried
unto my
GOD.
He... ...above,
He took... ...drew me
out of
many waters.
Ps. 18.

Author of the hymn "Throw Out the Lifeline," the
Rev. Edwin S. Ufford stands in his ship's-prow pulpit
in the Galilee Temple in Rockland, backed by the
symbols that promised salvation for those in peril
on the sea: a lighthouse, a painting of Christ walking
on water, and biblical quotations. (Fig. 43)

Beginning to sink
he cried, saying,
LORD
save me!
And immediately
JESUS
Stretched forth
his hand
and
caught him.
Mat. 14.

44

45

46

47

48

49

50

51

52

A lighthouse is often the proud emblem of the agencies that protect the physical and spiritual well-being of Maine's coastal citizens.

NOËL ~ ALL'S WELL

U.S. COAST GUARD

Detail of *Seascape with Lighthouse*.
Charles Codman, 1837.

"Steadfast, Serene, Immovable"

The Maine Lighthouse in American Art

Thomas Andrew Denenberg

2

Images of the Maine coast have long enjoyed great currency in American visual culture. Trading on age-old artistic conventions, nineteenth-century marine painters created an industry out of the tradition of supplying images of the sea in its many moods. Over time, these scenes—from quiescent harbors at dawn to the frothy drama of waves breaking offshore—gained favor in the popular imagination and have come to represent the region in the canon of American art. The symbols that make up an iconography of the Maine coast have proven to be persistent and persuasive—sky, sea, waves, headlands, islands, rocks, and generations of vessels both proud and doomed. But above all one immediately recognizable part of the built environment has remained richly important to the coastal scene—the lighthouse. From grand romantic views of the nineteenth century to the cool authority of Modernist watercolors, images of lighthouses play a key role in defining Maine.

Paintings of lighthouses have a long and distinguished history. As Dutch artists of the seventeenth century valorized the men and ships that built and sustained their thriving economy, the act of including the lantern of Genoa or an idealized Mediterranean lighthouse served

Edward Hopper painting *Lighthouse Hill*, at Two Lights near Cape Elizabeth, Maine, 1927. © The Arthayer R. Sanborn Hopper Collection Trust—2005 (above).

3

Charles Codman. *Seascape with Lighthouse*. 1837.
Delaware Art Museum, Bequest of Elizabeth Wales, 1951.

as a marker of worldly knowledge. With England ruling the waves in the eighteenth century, romantic visions of storm-tossed merchantmen guided to safe harbor by a shaft of light from a granite tower came to represent the sublime thrill of maritime adventure. It fell to the United States, a young nation intimately tied to the ocean, to embed the image of the lighthouse in a recognizable iconology and to develop coherent and lasting meaning for the symbol in both image and text.

Art historian David Miller has examined the ways that American character was shaped by the language of maritime peril over the centuries. Beginning with John Winthrop's 1630 assertion on board the *Arabella* that a breached Puritan covenant with God can best be described in terms of a shipwreck, followed by descriptions in the Early Republic of the many dangers foreign powers posed to the "ship of state," and on to Daniel Webster's defense of the Compromise of 1850 as avoiding dashing the new nation on the rocks, cultural fears were often expressed in terms of catastrophic navigational error at sea.[1] Lighthouses, both real and imagined, thus were held in high esteem.

Thomas Doughty. *Desert Rock Lighthouse*. 1847.
Newark Museum, Gift of Mrs. Jennie E. Mead, 1939.

Seascape with Lighthouse by Charles Codman is an archetype of marine painting in the Early Republic. A Portland resident, Codman (1800/1–1842) has long been identified as a seminal figure in the creative culture of Maine as he rose above the role of sign painter and architectural decorator and began to offer easel paintings for sale in the late 1820s.[2] *Seascape with Lighthouse* owes a debt to the earlier Dutch and English traditions of maritime painting and perhaps was based on an engraving or a pastiche of prints. This romantic painting reduces to essentials the view, setting up a timeless narrative of the stalwart beacon rising above the waves, rather than depicting any one specific Maine lighthouse.

Codman was far from alone in taking liberties when it came to composing scenes that demonstrated the grandeur of nature on the coast in the first half of the nineteenth century. Thomas Doughty (1793–1856), a Philadelphia native, moved to Boston in 1832 and began painting the northern frontier of Maine the following year. In 1836 and 1847 he produced imaginative canvases bearing the same title, *Desert Rock Lighthouse*, that combine features of the 1830 lighthouse on Mount

Nathaniel Currier and James Merritt Ives. *American Coast Scene, Desert Rock Lighthouse.* Nineteenth century. © Shelburne Museum, Shelburne, Vermont.

Desert Rock with the setting of Egg Rock, a distinctive geological feature.[3] Such artistic license was typical of American landscape painters—and of centuries of European painters. But Doughty's vision achieved widespread acceptance when his paintings served as the basis of a Currier and Ives lithograph in the 1860s. Currier and Ives, taking advantage of new printing technologies, offered Doughty's view of the wild coast, endangered ship, and constant beacon as generic coastal scene. The translation of Doughty's work by this lithograph not only demonstrates the liberties taken during the process, but stands as an indication of popular taste among the rising industrial middle class.

Although the dramatic imaginative sublimity captured by Codman, Doughty, and Currier and Ives never left the stage in America, other modes of visual expression found favor in the mid-nineteenth century, including a school of painting that promoted quiescence typified by the work of Fitz Henry Lane (1804–1865). A native of Gloucester, Massachusetts, Lane enjoyed

Mount Desert Rock Light, Maine.

When compared with this postcard view of Mount Desert Rock Light, the Currier and Ives print based on Thomas Doughty's painting of the same lighthouse reveals the artistic license that was typical of American landscape painters.

popular success in his lifetime and proved to be a prolific artist specializing in images of quiet coastal commerce. In 1848, Lane made the first of many trips to Maine to paint, eventually visiting Castine, Camden, Penobscot Bay, Blue Hill, and Mount Desert Island.[4] John Wilmerding noted that Lane was the first painter to employ "stilled time" as a method for expressing a mood.[5] This interest in calm seas and snug harbors not only provided comfort for the men aboard ship, but also those who invested in shipping—not coincidentally the same individuals who collected paintings at the time. Lane's paintings promoted a national image of steady commercial activity in an era of rapid social and economic modernization. His depiction of lighthouses—especially those he encountered and documented on his trips to the coast of Maine—are part of his aesthetic and ideology of quiet national success. A great maritime nation naturally required infrastructure to support commerce, and lighthouses played an important role in Lane's work, as they did in the growing American economy.

Fitz Henry Lane. *Owl's Head, Penobscot Bay, Maine.* 1862.
Photograph © 2012 Museum of Fine Arts, Boston.

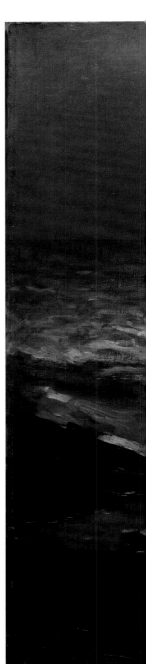

8

Published by V. T. Shaw   Winslow Homer Studio, Prout's Neck, Me.

9

Winslow Homer. *Wild Geese in Flight*. 1897.
Portland Museum of Art, Maine.

Winslow Homer. *Moonlight, Wood Island Light*. 1894.
Image copyright © The Metropolitan Museum of Art /
Art Resource, New York.

The impact of modernity on the American scene—captured with such cool authority by Fitz Henry Lane—was lessened by a sense of ambiguity by the turn of the century. As industrialization and urbanization forever changed the pace of life, artists such as Winslow Homer (1836–1910) sought solace on the coast of Maine as part of a national search for authenticity. Although Homer occasionally included the beacon of a lighthouse in his work—witness *Moonlight, Wood Island Light* of 1894—his most chilling portrayal of the effects of a lighthouse, titled *Wild Geese in Flight*, tellingly erases the structure. Originally called *At the Base of the Lighthouse*, the painting is testimony to the unpredictable nature of modern life as the unseen navigational aid has unintentionally proven to be as fatal as birdshot for the downed geese on the dunes.

Edward Hopper. *Captain Strout's House, Portland Head.* 1927.
Image copyright © Wadsworth Atheneum Museum of Art /
Art Resource, New York.

Homer's commitment to the coast of Maine not only produced some of the greatest modern interpretations of the timeless drama of wave on rock, but also provided inspiration for a generation of painters who followed him in the twentieth century. Edward Hopper (1882–1967)—one of the most famous to take up the task of painting the coast—first came to Maine during World War I and returned on a number of occasions. In 1927, he purchased an automobile and made a survey of the lighthouses at Cape Elizabeth. His watercolors of Portland Head Light and Two Lights stand as monuments of American culture. A master of creating inflection using little more than the effect of light and shadow, Hopper also paid close attention to composition. On a number of occasions he chose to truncate his lighthouses—to cut them off and depict them without a beacon in an effort to render Maine and New England without activity, quiet, and from another era. In doing so, he participated in the twentieth-century construction of Maine as a timeless place to rest rather than engage in commerce.

Edward Hopper. *The Lighthouse at Two Lights*. 1929.
Image copyright © The Metropolitan Museum of Art /
Art Resource, New York.

13

14

Yasuo Kuniyoshi. *The Swimmer*. c. 1924.
Columbus Museum of Art, Ohio.
Art © Estate of Yasuo Kuniyoshi /
Licensed by VAGA, New York.

Modernist Maine proved to be highly respectful of traditional symbols such as the lighthouse. Yasuo Kuniyoshi (1889–1953) immigrated to the United States in 1906 and soon came to the attention of Hamilton Easter Field, who brought the young man to Ogunquit to paint. There, Kuniyoshi reveled in the talismans of local culture that Field collected, including weathervanes, decoys, and nineteenth-century portraits and painted furniture. It is hard to miss the influence of Kuniyoshi's eye for folk art in *The Swimmer* of around 1924. The island lighthouse and keeper's residence are clearly references to Nubble Light off Cape Neddick, though like so many who came before him, Kuniyoshi incorporates features from many lighthouses in his painting. Marsden Hartley (1877–1943), a Maine native who made his career when he returned to his home state and began exploring native themes, captured the tumult of the world in which he lived when he produced *The Lighthouse* in 1940–41. On the eve of America's entrance into World War II, a global conflict of unprecedented proportion, Hartley's lighthouse is off-kilter, but standing resolutely among rocks and waves so large they reach the clouds.

15

Warren Gould Roby (attributed). Weathervane. 1850–1875.
© Shelburne Museum, Shelburne, Vermont.

16

Marsden Hartley. *The Lighthouse*. 1940–41.
Collection of J. R. and Barbara Hyde.

17

Andrew Wyeth. *Sailor's Valentine*. 1985.
Private Collection. ©Andrew Wyeth.

Postwar America was a time and place of prosperity and quiescence, but in New England, economic slow-down intensified the region's reputation as venerable, even timeless, and engendered a culture of tourism that proved attractive to artists and their patrons. Monhegan Island off the coast of Port Clyde—long a haven for painters and photographers—became a *de rigueur* stop for both rusticating Modernists and traditionalists looking to capture the "old" New England scene. As abstraction achieved hegemony in American art, a counter spin emanated from mid-coast Maine in the work of Andrew Wyeth (1917–2009). The son of N. C. Wyeth (1882–1945)—by leagues the most famous illustrator of his day—the younger Wyeth adopted traditional materials and techniques and placed his skills in the service of a new school of figurative painting that injected a cool light into American visual culture and perfectly captured a sense of national mood during the cold war. He also begat Jamie Wyeth (born 1946)—the third generation of what has become the country's first family of painters. Jamie,

responding to the profound changes in American culture of the 1960s and 1970s, developed an eye for the curious coincidences of life on the Maine coast. While his father was willing to narrate but leave the moral untold in his art, Jamie heightens the complexities and contradictions of the New England scene—a wild-haired figure in an eighteenth-century military coat standing in front of a whitewashed lighthouse or the behavior of seagulls considered against the same backdrop provoke thoughts of history, nature, and the iconoclastic coast of Maine.

As a powerful symbol within the history of American art, the Maine lighthouse has stunning staying power. From the Early Republic to the Modern era, artists have found inspiration in these utilitarian structures, so much so that they have become a part of the mythic landscape of the Pine Tree State. A symbol of hope, refuge, and constancy, lighthouses have been read in religious terms and painted in secular light, but above all, they endure as part of the American scene.

Jamie Wyeth. *Comet*. 1997.
© Jamie Wyeth.

Jamie Wyeth. *Lighthouse*. 1993.
© Jamie Wyeth.

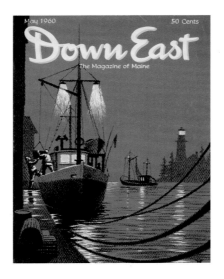

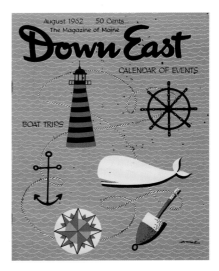

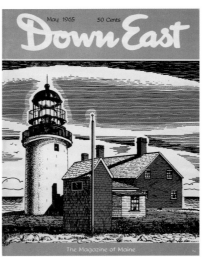

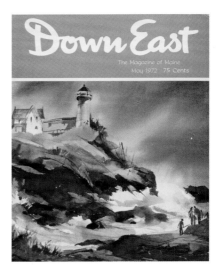

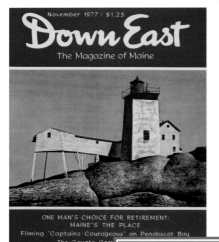

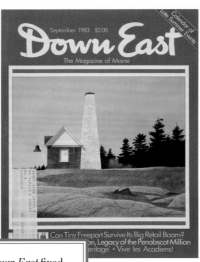

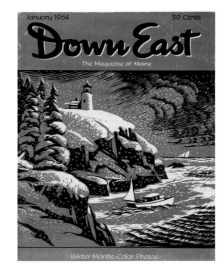

Magazines such as *Down East* fixed the popular image of Maine's lighthouses in the American imagination.

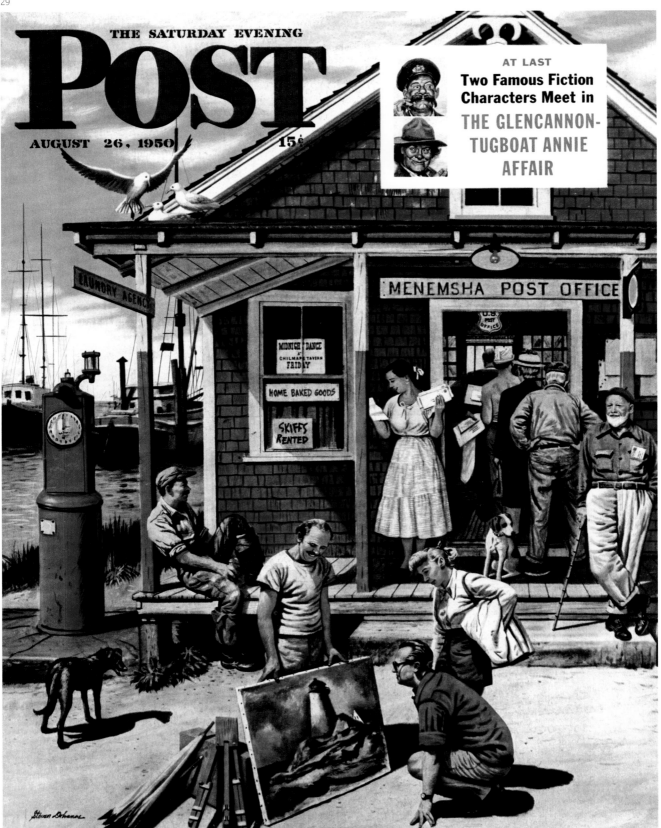

Stevan Dohanos. *Saturday Evening Post*. August 26, 1950.
Illustration © SEPS licensed by Curtis Licensing,
Indianapolis, Indiana. All rights reserved.

1

Active from 1877 to 1896, fashionably dressed
John F. Singhi of Rockland was one of many
Maine photographers who made pictures of the
state's lighthouses in the years after the Civil War.

Frozen in Time

The Photography of Maine's Lighthouses

Earle G. Shettleworth, Jr.

2

From the eve of the Civil War to the present, the lighthouses of Maine's extended coastline have been a favorite subject for photographers. The daguerreotype, the earliest form of popular photography, arrived in Maine in 1840, but the first known lighthouse photograph was not taken until 1858. On August 3 of that year, the Venerable Cunner Association, a Portland social club, held a summer outing at Portland Head Light in Cape Elizabeth. During this gathering, twenty-three members assembled to face an unknown photographer with the keeper's house and light tower figuring prominently in the background (see pages 148–49).

The newly available technology of glass negative and paper print used to create this 1858 picture was employed the next year by Portland photographer William H. McLaughlin when he was commissioned by the federal government to photograph all of Maine's coastal lighthouses, probably for record-keeping purposes. Of the forty-three lights active at the time, McLaughlin is known to have visited forty-two, Pond Island being the possible exception. Two sets of these pictures survive, one in the National Archives and the other in the U. S. Coast Guard Archives. The Maine Historic Preservation Commission owns four original prints as well. The extensive territory that McLaughlin covered in 1859, coupled with the physical challenges that he must have encountered, make this group of images all the more remarkable. Transcending his initial charge of photographically recording federal property, McLaughlin captured the first portraits of Maine light stations, giving an uncompromising view of their construction, both crude and finished, as well as their harsh topography peopled by the brave individuals who operated them.

Gathered for an outing at Portland Head Light, members of the Venerable Cunner Association face the camera in this earliest known photographic image of a Maine lighthouse, taken on August 3, 1858. It was made using the latest technology of glass negative and paper. Other methods, such as the daguerreotype or the ambrotype (like the image of a mariner shown at right), were more suitable for making studio portraits than for shooting outdoor scenes. (Figs. 3, 4)

5

1st Dist. Photos

Deer Island Thorofare
Lt. Sta.

6

Whitehead Lt.

7

8

1st Dist.

Hendricks Head Lt. Sta., Me.

9

William McLaughlin's photographs offer a time capsule of Maine's lighthouses in 1859. The lights shown here are (6–9): Pemaquid Point, Deer Island Thoroughfare, Whitehead, Cape Elizabeth, and Hendrick's Head.

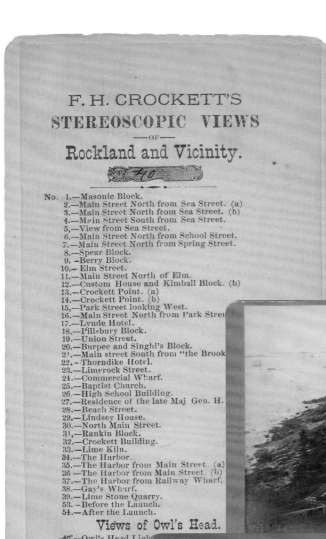

F. H. CROCKETT'S
STEREOSCOPIC VIEWS
—OF—
Rockland and Vicinity.
No. 40

No. 1.—Masonic Block.
2.—Main Street North from Sea Street. (a)
3.—Main Street North from Sea Street. (b)
4.—Main Street South from Sea Street.
5,—View from Sea Street.
6.—Main Street North from School Street.
7.—Main Street North from Spring Street.
8.—Spear Block.
9.—Berry Block.
10.—Elm Street.
11.—Main Street North of Elm.
12.—Custom House and Kimball Block. (b)
13.—Crockett Point. (a)
14.—Crockett Point. (b)
15.—Park Street looking West.
16.—Main Street North from Park Street.
17.—Lynde Hotel.
18.—Pillsbury Block.
19.—Union Street.
20.—Burpee and Singhi's Block.
21.—Main street South from "the Brook."
22.—Thorndike Hotel.
23.—Limerock Street.
24.—Commercial Wharf.
25.—Baptist Church.
26.—High School Building.
27.—Residence of the late Maj Gen. H.
28.—Beach Street.
29.—Lindsey House.
30.—North Main Street.
31,—Rankin Block.
32.—Crockett Building.
33.—Lime Kiln.
34.—The Harbor.
35.—The Harbor from Main Street. (a)
36.—The Harbor from Main Street. (b)
37.—The Harbor from Railway Wharf.
38.—Gay's Wharf.
39.—Lime Stone Quarry.
53.—Before the Launch.
54.—After the Launch.

Views of Owl's Head.

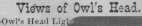

40.—Owl's Head Light
41.—Owl's Head from
42.—Owl's Head from
43.—Owl's Head from
44.—View West from
45.—Owl's Head from
46.—Ocean House, O
47.—Ocean House, O
48.—"Mine Host" of
49.—Entrance to Ow
50.—The Beach at O
51.—The Beach at O
52.—Ledge and Harb

10

11

Rockbound lighthouses were great subjects for the three-dimensional images produced by stereo views when seen through a stereoscope. Photographers like F. H. Crockett of Rockland, who recorded Owl's Head (above), and J. Henry Allen of South Thomaston, who shot the two towers on Matinicus Rock (at right), frequently printed lists of available views on the backs of their cards.

12

14

15

After the Civil War, Maine landscape photography became more widespread, its popularity due in part to the growing number of summer visitors who wanted modestly priced pictorial souvenirs by which to remember the Maine coast. Local photographers met this need by producing large numbers of stereo views, cabinet photographs, and individual prints that were mounted in albums or kept in folios. Of the stereo views made of Maine lights between 1865 and 1900, cards of Matinicus Rock by the South Thomaston photographer J. Henry Allen stand out for their stark depiction of one of the coast's most remote locations. In these 1877 views, one or both of the twin granite towers rise defiantly from the island's unforgiving rocky surface, while the figures of men, women, and children populate this forbidding environment. On a lighter note is the Augusta photographer Henry Bailey's stereo view of tourists visiting Monhegan Island Light about 1880. A large group is assembled at the base of the tower with others crowded on the deck of the lantern (see page 175). During this period, notable cabinet views of Dice's Head Light were issued by the Boston photographer Augustine H. Folsom, and Frank Weston of Bangor took a memorable large-format photograph of Mount Desert Rock and its inhabitants.

This 1880s cabinet view of Dice's Head Light is one of many photographs of the Castine area taken by Augustine H. Folsom, a Boston photographer who summered in Castine. (Fig. 16)

In the 1880s, Maine lighthouse photography was taken to a new level of artistry by Henry G. Peabody, a professional landscape and marine photographer working in Boston from 1886 to 1900. Peabody employed his talented eye and finely honed technical skills to create striking images of Maine lighthouses and related coastal scenery. His photographs found a ready market as individual mounted prints and as illustrations for tourist brochures such as *Souvenir of York Beach*, which he self-published in 1888, and *New England's Seashore*, which was distributed by the Boston and Maine Railroad about 1890.

Peabody's photographic tribute to the Maine coast is embodied in an elaborate oblong folio volume entitled *The Coast of Maine*, which he published in Boston in 1889. This book traces a journey from Campobello in New Brunswick to the Isles of Shoals in Maine and New Hampshire through the words of such New England literary figures as James Russell Lowell and Celia Thaxter as well as in fifty full-page photographic plates by Peabody. Sixteen of these plates depict Maine lights from West Quoddy Head to Boon Island. Original prints of these and other Maine lighthouses taken by Peabody are now owned by the Maine Historic Preservation Commission, the Peabody Essex Museum, Historic New England, and the University of California.

Herbert Bamber, a civil engineer and photographer with the U. S. Light-House Establishment, worked on assignment in Maine in the early 1890s to record all of the state's lighthouses. Many of his original blue-tinted cyanotype prints survive, but like this fine view of Petit Manan, they are usually reproduced in black-and-white.

19

Henry G. Peabody's collection of views in the *The Coast of Maine* includes this wonderfully stark photograph of Pond Island Light. (Fig. 20)

21

22

23

Another noted Boston commercial photographer, Nathaniel L. Stebbins (above), approached the use of Maine lighthouse photographs in a different way from Peabody. The development of photolithography in the 1880s made it possible to photographically illustrate publications, and Stebbins took advantage of this new technology to publish *The Illustrated Coast Pilot* in Boston in 1891. So popular was this navigational handbook that it went through at least eight printings between 1891 and 1909. Stebbins followed the Maine coast from the New Hampshire line to the Canadian border. In contrast to Peabody, he included pictures of most of the light stations and other navigational aids, placed their photographs four to a page, and provided legibility rather than artistry in the reproduction quality of his plates. Here was the difference between lighthouse photography in the service of aesthetics versus practicality.

While Nathaniel Stebbins's *The Illustrated Coast Pilot* was intended for use by serious mariners, two early twentieth-century brochures issued by the Maine Steamship Company were more recreational in nature. *Light Houses along the Coast between Portland and New York* and its second edition, *Lighthouses and Lightships by Sea to Maine*, were intended to help passengers on deck identify navigational landmarks on trips between Portland Harbor and New York Harbor. The photographs for these pamphlets were furnished by Stebbins and were reproduced in a format and quality similar to those in his *The Illustrated Coast Pilot*. But the same subject in the *Pilot* can be represented by a slightly different image in the steamship brochures.

376½ miles from New York   13½ miles from Por
CAPE ELIZABETH LIGHTSHIP, ME.

382 miles from New York   8 miles from Po
CAPE ELIZABETH LIGHTS, ME.

386½ miles from New York   3½ miles from Po
PORTLAND HEAD (entrance to Harbor)

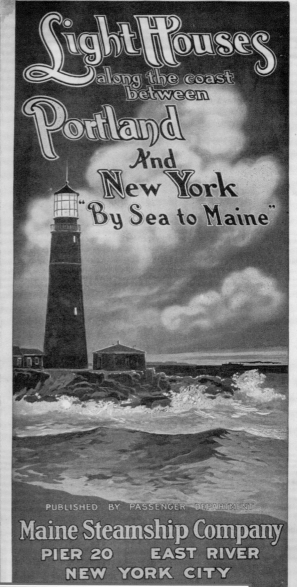

388 miles from New York   1½ miles from Portland
SPRING POINT LIGHT (Portland Harbor)

A yachtsman as well as a commercial photographer, Nathaniel L. Stebbins specialized not only in shooting coastal scenes but also in taking pictures of the many sailing and steam vessels that frequented Boston Harbor during the late nineteenth and early twentieth centuries.

Casco Bay, Maine., Half-way Rock Light.

The painterly quality of the color lithographic postcards printed in Germany for Maine firms is evident in the view of Halfway Rock Light at left and the image of Bass Harbor Head Light that appears on the next two pages, published by the Hugh C. Leighton Company. (Fig. 29)

In 1898 Congress passed the private mailing act to promote the growth of the fledgling American postcard industry. Stereo views and photographic prints were quickly supplanted in popularity as tourist items by the new picture postcard. Overnight, sending and collecting postcards became a national craze, resulting in the establishment of two major early twentieth-century publishers in Portland, Maine: the Hugh C. Leighton Company, which became Leighton & Valentine in 1910, and the George W. Morris Company. Prior to World War I, both of these concerns relied heavily on German printers to produce high-quality color lithographic cards. While Morris carried a selection of Maine lighthouse views, Leighton produced cards of at least forty-eight Maine light stations, several of them using Nathaniel Stebbins's photographs. Leighton's interest in lighthouse views is reflected in the descriptive paragraphs that appear on the backs of many of the cards as well as in their outstanding color quality, in some cases reaching the level of a fine period painting. That the public collected these lighthouse cards is found in a handwritten message on the reverse of a Leighton view of the Cuckolds (above), in which the writer says to the recepient, "I thought perhaps you would like this view in your collection."

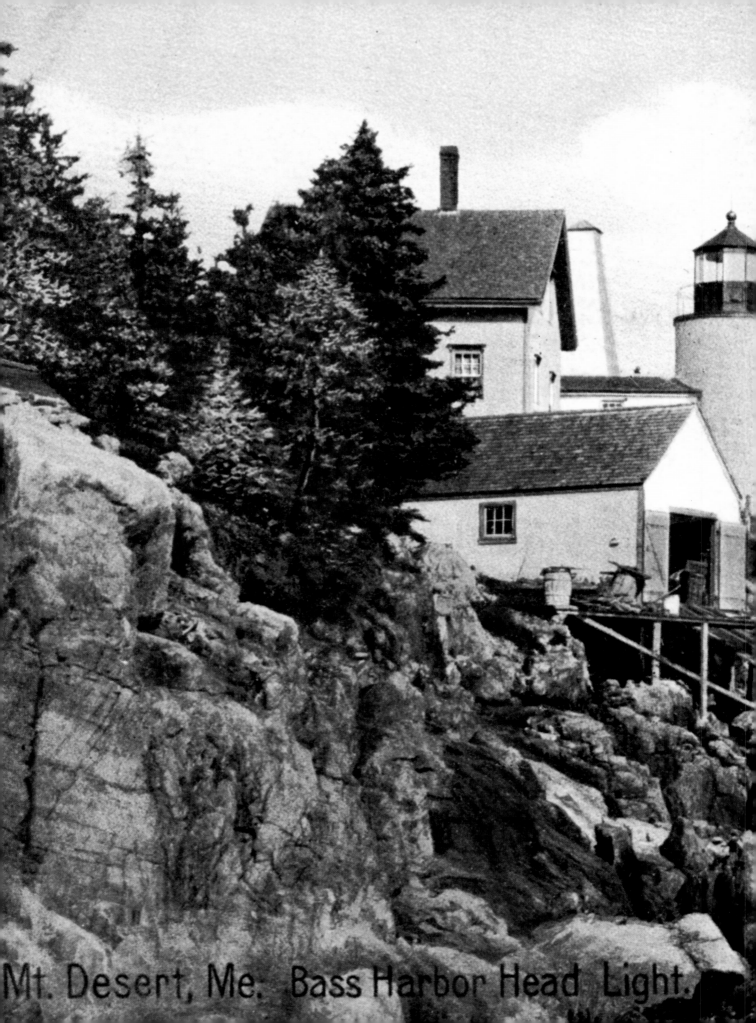

Mt. Desert, Me. Bass Harbor Head Light.

BRACKETT

30

LABBIE

33

BALLARD

32

BLOOD

31

McDOUGALL AND KEEFE

34

Individual photographers who issued real photo postcards of the most popular lighthouses, such as Portland Head and Monhegan Island as seen above, competed with large firms like the Eastern Illustrating & Publishing Company that produced postcards of almost every light station in Maine.

35

36

37

World War I brought about a greater reliance on domestically made postcards and gave a boost to the production of quality real photo postcards, which were printed directly from glass negatives usually taken by professional photographers. The leading maker of real photo postcards of Maine lighthouses was the Eastern Illustrating & Publishing Company, which was founded in Belfast by R. Herman Cassens. Between 1909 and 1947 Eastern Illustrating sold cards of many of Maine's lights, and the clarity and detail of these views make them a valuable reference.

During the first half of the twentieth century, Eastern Illustrating was not alone in producing significant real photo postcards of Maine lighthouses, especially the two most popular ones, Portland Head Light and Monhegan Island Light. Photographers Harvard M. Armstrong, W. H. Ballard, J. Carleton Bicknell, Ralph F. Blood, Edwin L. Inness, and Leroy N. Mitchell produced fine views of that emblematic Cape Elizabeth Light known around the world. Similarly, Lorimer E. Brackett, Joseph A. Labbie, Josephine Davis Townsend, and the partnership of McDougall and Keefe were responsible for cards of the granite tower atop Monhegan Island's Lighthouse Hill.

38

While the Historic American Buildings Survey was active in recording Maine landmarks in the 1930s, not until 1960 did the survey photograph its first lighthouse in the state. That year, architectural photographer Cervin Robinson made photographs of Saddleback Ledge Light for the H.A.B.S. collection at the Library of Congress, followed by Gerda Peterich's photographs of Breakwater Light in South Portland in 1962 and Jack Boucher's photographs of Portland Head Light in 1965.

After a hiatus of nearly a quarter of a century, the Maine Historic Preservation Commission significantly expanded the number of Maine lights recorded to H.A.B.S. standards. Using federal grants from the Bicentennial Lighthouse Fund, which was sponsored in Congress by Maine's Senator George Mitchell, the Commission hired the noted architectural photographer Richard Cheek in 1989 to make both exterior and interior views of forty-two light stations. Because of the ambitious scope of the project, Cheek divided the work over three seasons, completing the third phase in 1991. The results were a wealth of strikingly beautiful black-and-white images supplemented by an equally fine collection of color transparencies.

From William McLaughlin to Richard Cheek, each generation since the invention of photography has focused its cameras on the lighthouses of the Maine coast, resulting in a changing imagery reflective of its times and purposes. Yet the unaltered constant in all of this is the inseparable connection between the state's rugged coastline and its many lighthouses, made so evident through the artistry of photography. As the poet and writer Robert P. Tristram Coffin observed in his introduction to Robert Thayer Sterling's 1935 book *Lighthouses of the Maine Coast*:

They mean more than ornament and service, too. For they are connected with elemental eloquences, fire and wind and ancient worshipping. They are houses almost as holy as churches, in the long history of man.

Documentation of the Spring Point Ledge Light by Richard Cheek for the Historic American Buildings Survey in 1989 required the use of a 4 × 5 inch view camera to produce black-and-white negatives that were archivally processed for deposit at the Library of Congress.

Richard Cheek's view of the ocean side of Cape Neddick Light echoes Henry Peabody's photograph of Pond Island Light (see pages 158–59) by revealing the rocky cliffs that endangered any ship sailing too close in stormy or foggy weather. (Fig. 45)

1

JOURNEYS BEAUTIFUL
The Magazine of Travel

JUNE 1925
35¢

Alfred Trueman

MAINE NUMBER

Drawn to the Lights

How Lighthouses Became Maine's Greatest Tourist Attraction

David Richards

Cape Newagen, Me.
The Cuckolds

2

L ighthouses have become such prominent icons in the promotion of modern Maine tourism that it may be difficult to imagine a time when the navigational aids were oceanside sentinels for sailors rather than vantage points for visitors to Vacationland.

The evolution of lighthouses from guardians of the sea to landmarks of the tourist landscape was a gradual one that paralleled the development of tourism in Maine and that reflected, in turn, revolutions in transportation. Lighthouses dotted the coastline. This made them visible to steamship passengers, who were enjoying the best method of moving from one port to another prior to the Civil War. But the explosion of tourism that occurred after peace was declared was largely made possible by the proliferation of rail lines, first to coastal communi-ties and then inland toward the White Mountains of New Hampshire, the Canadian province of Quebec, and the cities along Maine's major rivers, the Androscoggin, Kennebec, and Penobscot. What ultimately made light-houses accessible and eventually iconic was the mobility provided to tourists by the automobile.

In the twentieth century, the ephemera of tourism promotion seized upon the structures not only as sites to see, but also as the quintessential symbol to signify the state of Maine. Because the lights could now be viewed close up from the land rather than at a distance from the sea, the prospect of lighthouses silhouetted against ocean and horizon became much more dramatic, drawing attention away from the traditional scenes of "fish and forest" and "moose and mountains" that had

3

The new medium of photography recorded the popularity of lighthouses as tourist attractions. Lithographs based on photographic images became staples of souvenir booklets such as *Beacon Lights*.

been serving as the Pine Tree State's main attractions. "Lobsters and lighthouses" became the dominant image instead.

When the first tourist visited a Maine lighthouse is unknown. The first photographic record dates to 1858, when members of a local social club gathered for an outing and group shot at Portland Head Light (see pages 148–49). What is clear is that by the mid-nineteenth century, lighthouses had attracted so much public curiosity that the 1853 *Instructions for Lighthouse Keepers* included suggestions for dealing with uninvited guests. Keepers could show strangers around, so long as it was during daylight and did not interfere with operations. Under no circumstances should the public be allowed to touch the equipment. The foremost charge to the keepers was to be polite. Visitation steadily increased, causing new instructions to be issued that closed lighthouses to guests on Sundays, set regular visiting hours on Tuesdays through Fridays, and granted keepers more latitude to bend the rules according to circumstances.

4

5

HERE AND THERE
IN NEW ENGLAND AND CANADA.
BY THE
BOSTON AND
MAINE R·R·

ALL ALONG SHORE.

Cape Elizabeth, Me., Portland Head Light and Cliffs.

KENNEBUNKPORT RIVER

OLD ORCHARD BEACH,
LOOKING NORTH.

OLD ORCHARD BEACH,
LOOKING SOUTH

SCE...
GE...

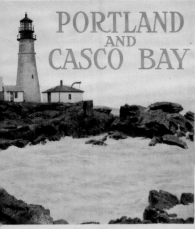

PORTLAND
AND
CASCO BAY

Mercy to Mother.

Portland Light, Me.

Harlow

Range 11¾ miles, erected 1790, 101 feet above the level of the sea, ceded to the government 1796_
In 1883 the height was reduced to 80 feet thus changing it from a 2nd to 4th grade_
Argand lamps used.

Copyright 1885.

9

White Head,
Portland Harbor.

Nowhere fairer, sweeter, rarer,
Does the golden-locked fruit-bearer,
Through his painted woodlands stray,
Than where hillside oaks and beeches
Overlook the long blue reaches,
Silver coves and pebbled beaches,
And green isles of Casco Bay;
Nowhere day, for delay,
With a tenderer look beseeches,
"Let me with my charmed earth stay,"
J G Whittier

From the pleasant paths I used to tread
Full many a mile away,
I dream of the rocks of old White Head,
And the billows of Casco Bay.
I sit once more on the
Where the waves dash
And listen again their
As the murmurous
E A Allen

PORTLAND LIGHT

SKETCHES AT
PORTLAND, ME.
ON THE
BOSTON & MAINE
RAILROAD.

UNION STATION
PORTLAND

From the outset of travel promotion, the most iconic
of Maine's tourism symbols has been Portland Head
Light. For over a century, it has graced innumerable
postcards and covers to guides, maps, and books.
The light continues to possess the ideal blend of
location and lore to keep it one of Maine's leading
attractions in the twenty-first century.

10

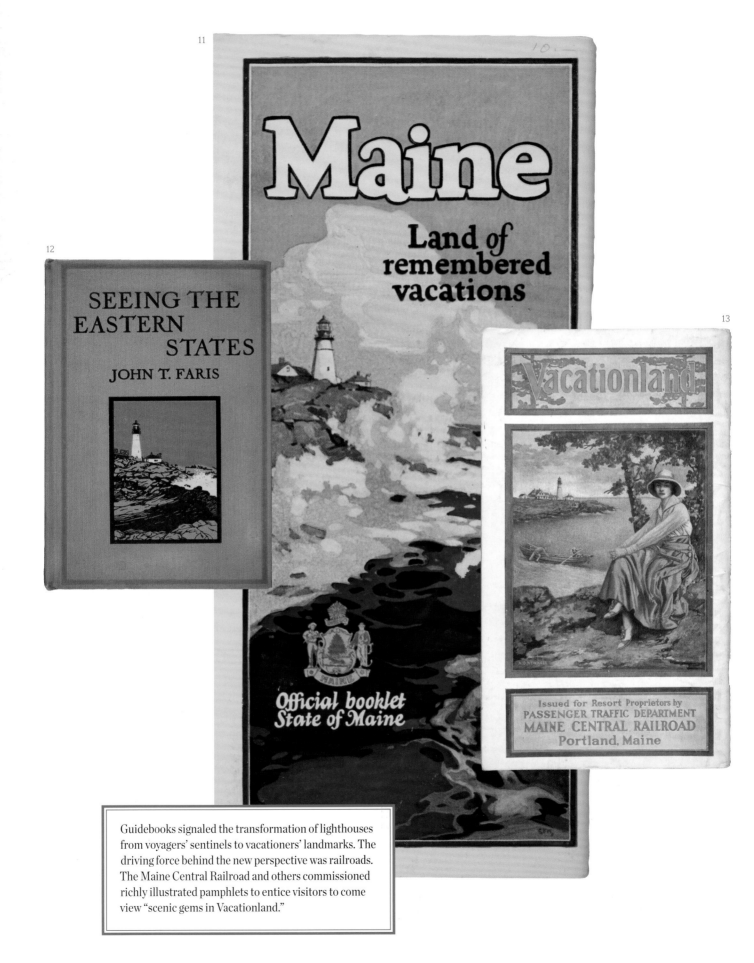

11

Maine

Land of remembered vacations

Official booklet
State of Maine

12

SEEING THE
EASTERN
STATES

JOHN T. FARIS

13

Vacationland

Issued for Resort Proprietors by
PASSENGER TRAFFIC DEPARTMENT
MAINE CENTRAL RAILROAD
Portland, Maine

Guidebooks signaled the transformation of lighthouses from voyagers' sentinels to vacationers' landmarks. The driving force behind the new perspective was railroads. The Maine Central Railroad and others commissioned richly illustrated pamphlets to entice visitors to come view "scenic gems in Vacationland."

Portland Head Light, Portland, Maine

14

The proximity of some lighthouses to coastal resorts made them irresistible attractions. For example, the Wassawinkeag, a summer hotel in Stockton Springs, was within easy walking distance of the Fort Point Light, and to the south, the Ocean House in Cape Elizabeth stood near Two Lights. But the leading light for tourism was Portland Head. It possesses several assets that have made it the most prominent lighthouse both geographically and imaginatively. First and foremost, it is favored by location, situated near Maine's most populous urban center, which gives it accessibility, and it also protects one of the most well-traveled sea routes into the port of Portland. Additionally, the setting is spectacular. The light sits on a promontory edged by a rocky shoreline upon which the surging ocean surf thunders persistently. According to one observer writing in 1881, "after storms many drive out to the Light to see the huge waves dash upon the shore." Portland Head's picturesque setting has captivated painters, photographers, and tourist promoters for nearly two centuries. Moreover, it has transformed the light into the most ubiquitous icon of the entire state.

Beyond its natural attributes, Portland Head's several appealing cultural characteristics further enhanced its popularity in the late nineteenth century. As Maine's first and oldest light, it possessed what passed for antiquity in a new nation. Its commission by President George Washington imbued it with historical significance as well as age. Association with notable shipwrecks lent an air of maritime romance to the site. Finally, lighthouses were beacons of technological innovation, full of delicate and precise equipment that had to be protected from curious visitors.

As the tourist industry in Maine took off during the last quarter of the nineteenth century, one of the state's premier promoters began to take note of the aesthetic and cultural features that gave lighthouses such great appeal to the traveling public. In *Picturesque Maine*, published in 1880, Moses Sweetser made mention of the "famous" Portland Head Light and the "tall revolving light" on Monhegan Island, as well as Seguin Island in Georgetown, "where a famous light-house crowns an insulated and fortress-like rock." Writing promotional copy for the Boston and Maine Railroad at the end of the decade, he touted the "modern" Nubble Lighthouse at Cape Neddick. Like Portland Head, it, too, sits on a rocky, wave-beaten promontory, close to the beaches of York. The far more remote Boon Island Light off the coast of York also fascinated Sweetser. There the modern marvel of the light contrasted with the mysterious "dark traditions" of cannibalism following a shipwreck a century and a half earlier.

15

16

17

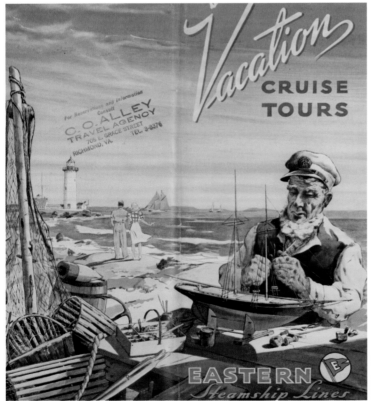

18

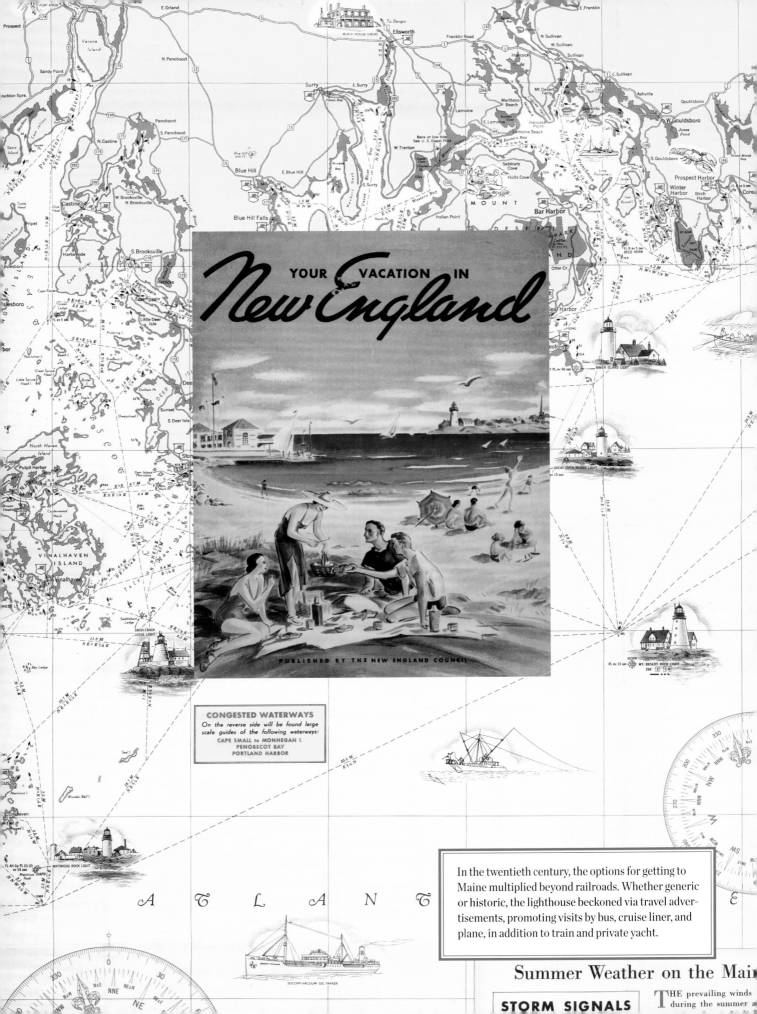

YOUR VACATION IN
New England

PUBLISHED BY THE NEW ENGLAND COUNCIL

CONGESTED WATERWAYS

On the reverse side will be found large scale guides of the following waterways:
CAPE SMALL to MONHEGAN I.
PENOBSCOT BAY
PORTLAND HARBOR

In the twentieth century, the options for getting to Maine multiplied beyond railroads. Whether generic or historic, the lighthouse beckoned via travel advertisements, promoting visits by bus, cruise liner, and plane, in addition to train and private yacht.

Summer Weather on the Mai

STORM SIGNALS

THE prevailing winds during the summer a

THE ATLA

21, 22

With the advent of the twentieth century, car travel began to supplant passage by train. Greater mobility afforded by roads over rail brought greater accessibility to lighthouses. A visit to one became almost obligatory during a Maine vacation. A photograph or two became a virtual requirement. The promotional machinery of the tourist trade and auto nation was quick to meet the demand. Publicity pamphlets illustrated the way to coastal lighthouses. Travel guides outlined routes where the navigational beacons beckoned. Maps provided graphic instruction. Through the Maine Publicity Bureau, the state began to take the lead in defining the destinations and images of Vacationland. Corporations involved in the travel industry quickly learned how to use lighthouses to promote their products and services. Along the way, lighthouses as a defining feature of the Maine tourist landscape gained national and even international audiences.

While lighthouses received plenty of publicity, what they needed to become true icons was popularity. They

needed to be personalized. In the middle of the twentieth century, authors began collecting the scattered stories that gave life to lighthouses. Published in 1929, *Lighthouses of New England* by Malcolm Willoughby endeavored "to collect the most interesting bits of history and legend." Six years later, Robert Thayer Sterling, assistant keeper of Portland Head Light, used his experience inside the United States Lighthouse Service to write *Lighthouses of the Maine Coast and the Men Who Keep Them*. The prime popularizer, however, was Edward Rowe Snow.

A prolific historian of maritime New England, Snow lent his personality to lighthouse lore by serving as the "Flying Santa" who delivered presents to keepers' families beginning in 1936 and continuing for more than four decades. In 1945, Yankee Publishing came out with Snow's *Famous New England Lighthouses*, a volume "packed with stories of danger and adventure which have befallen the men and women lighthouse keepers." The book was credited with providing "the impetus that launched an increase in lighthouse interest and preservation."

The automobile brought unparalleled mobility to the traveling public during the course of the twentieth century. As motorists took to the highways and byways of the nation, it was significant that many carmakers associated driving with the maritime symbol of navigational safety—the venerable lighthouse.

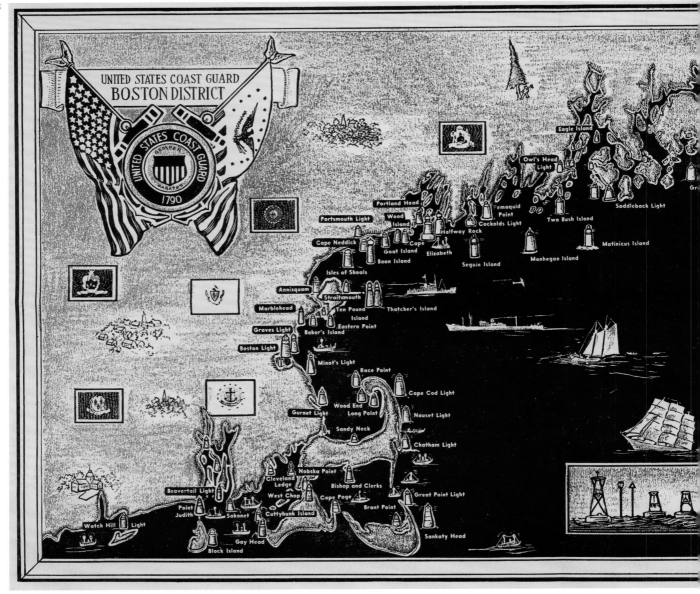

Far from descending into technological irrelevance, lighthouses have experienced a tourist renaissance as they have moved into a third century of service. Automation initially left the sites largely empty, although far from useless. Organizations such as the Island Institute and the American Lighthouse Foundation were formed to help preserve the light stations that were being vacated by the Coast Guard. New public uses as parks, museums, and even accommodations were found for the suddenly lifeless sentinels. The era of automation actually made them more accessible; consequently, even more people have been drawn to the lights in the twenty-first century.

Visitors can now take in lighthouses the way they were originally viewed, via the sea without having to board an ocean liner. Local coastline cruises to see the lights are offered by such organizations as the American Lighthouse Foundation and the Maine Maritime Museum in Bath as well as by commercial operators. Lighthouse aficionados can also look down on the sentinels of the sea from planes operated by regional aviation companies.

Even before entering museums or boarding boats or planes, tourists can come prepared with reams of information. Scores of state maps, regional magazines, travel books, tourist guides, internet printouts, and newspaper supplements cover every aspect imaginable about Maine's iconic beacons of maritime heritage. There are also a good number of lighthouse histories available, in-

Books devoted to the history and lore of lighthouses have helped to increase popular nostalgia for the sentinels. Among the most important mid-twentieth-century promoters of the romance of lighthouses was author and "Flying Santa," Edward Rowe Snow.

cluding Down East Press's *Lighthouses of Maine* (1986) by noted Maine journalist Bill Caldwell and the definitive, encyclopedic *The Lighthouses of Maine* (2009) by Jeremy D'Entremont, official historian for the American Lighthouse Foundation.

What accounts for the enduring popularity of Maine lighthouses? There are the aesthetic reasons—their simple beauty and stately utility make them highly photogenic and supremely functional. There is the romantic allure provided by enthralling tales of tragedy and ill-fated shipwrecks, interspersed with dramatic accounts of perilous rescues. There is the appeal of constancy, of steadfastly shining rays of clarity into impenetrable fog banks, both literal and figurative, both climatological

and cultural. There is the power of durability, of solidly and stolidly weathering decades of pounding surf and howling gales, and in some instances, the alarms of warfare too. Finally, for a nation fully invested in the Puritan ideal of constructing a shining "City Upon a Hill," lighthouses have come to serve as beacons of individual liberty and personal opportunity for the rest of the world. This accumulation of qualities embodied in towers of brick, stone, cement, and metal likely will continue to draw pilgrims to the lights and will sustain lighthouses as Maine's greatest tourist attraction throughout the twenty-first century, and well beyond.

This colorful array of books and ephemera demonstrates the modern mania for Maine lighthouses, which has become a niche unto itself for tourists and collectors alike. It also shows how visitors continue to be drawn to the lights to this day. (Fig. 31)

Beacons for Business

The Commercial Use of the Lighthouse Image

Richard Cheek

2

Even if a visitor to Maine does not go to see any lighthouses while he's there, he will leave with a lighter wallet because of their presence. Beyond being promoted as the state's foremost tourist attraction, the lights have been transformed for commercial purposes by entrepreneurs in three main ways: as the signature image for printed advertisements and company trademarks, as landlocked replicas to attract attention to roadside businesses, and as gifts and collectibles that follow the form or bear the image of a tapered tower with a lantern on top.

The use of the lighthouse as the main graphic device in printed advertisements is as time-tested as many of the beacons that line Maine's coast. Because the hazards of coastal navigation were so well known and the fear of and fascination with shipwrecks was so widespread, the construction of the stations and the heroics of the lightkeeping and lifesaving services were well publicized right from their start. By the second half of the nineteenth century, the public was very familiar with what most of the lights looked like because their images were appearing in American art and photography, nautical books and adventure tales, children's literature, travel guides, and national magazines and newspapers. And people admired the many virtues that had come to be associated with the lighthouses: durability, steadfastness, dependability, courage, faithfulness, devotion to others, and the like. It was inevitable that such an eye-catching,

3

4

5

storied, and revered symbol would be seized upon by advertisers for use in promoting commercial products, even if the products themselves were seldom deserving of the same respect.

Colored trade cards were one of the earliest forms of advertisement to carry images of individual lighthouses. As giveaways that accompanied products such as processed food or tobacco, they were issued in series in order to encourage additional purchases, beginning in the 1870s. Other products were given labels with lighthouses on them, such as match boxes, implying that the matches would never fail to light when struck, or Lighthouse Cleanser, suggesting to the buyer that the powder would enable her to keep her house as spic and span as a lighthouse. But the association could be farfetched, as it was when S. H. Ransom & Company of Albany, New York, named its latest potbellied heating stove "The Light House" in 1872.

The stormy or peaceful lighthouse scenes featured on trade cards often had nothing to do with the products they advertised, such as overcoats and suits, pianos and organs, or patent medicines.

ROOFING

The
BEACON
LIGHT
to a GOOD
COMPLEXION

A shining countenance is produced by ordinary soaps. The use of Pears' reflects beauty and refinement. Pears' leaves the skin soft, white and natural.
Matchless for the Complexion.

OF ALL SCENTED SOAPS PEARS' OTTO OF ROSE IS THE BEST.
"*All rights secured.*"

WARNER'S
SAFE
YEAST

BE GUIDED BY THIS BEACON LIGHT,
YOUR HEALTHFUL COURSE WILL E'ER BE RIGHT.

INDIGESTION

BAD HEALTH

Although lighthouses were more commonly used as branding symbols on labels, they were sometimes transformed into the product itself, such as a giant roll of rubber roofing, a stack of soap boxes, or a massive can of yeast, each with a beaming lantern on top. (Figs. 10–14)

Instantly access enterprise-wide information, and you're out of the woods.

15

In order to reach the widest possible audience, most ads featuring lighthouses were placed in newspapers and magazines. With a fanciful or manipulative turn of mind, almost any product could be pushed, from soup and liquor to paints and cosmetics. Did you know that "like the lighthouses shining up and down our seacoast, Maxwell House is part of the American scene," or that Rollei cameras are "as dependable as a lighthouse"? Probably not, but it's surprising what some companies can teach you if you actually read their ads.

Of all the lights in Maine, Portland Head has been used the most to promote items such as Agfa Film, U. S. Savings Bonds, Chevrolet cars, B&M Baked Beans, Johnson Motors, and Coca Cola, just to name a few. It has also been the most altered: a local jewelry store buckled two Movado watches to the tower; Kellogg's painted the tower with red stripes and pretended the station was located on an island; and an IBM ad relocated it to the middle of a forest.

Johnson SEA-HORSE OUTBOARD MOTORS

Ideal for light housekeeping

"The best to you each morning"

Kellogg's CORN FLAKES

Best liked *(World's favorite)*
Best flavor *(Kellogg's secret)*
Worst to run out of *("Pick up a spare," says Yogi Bear)*

Chevrolet. Building a better way to see the U.S.A.

Our Chevelle Malibu Sport Coupe at Portland Head Light, Maine.

Chevelle for 1972. It fits more families, more budgets, more garages and more vacations.

It fits so well that in the last eight years it has become an American standard —a yardstick to measure how far your money can go. And how much comfort and room your money can buy.

Our Chevelle fits families so well, in size and price, it's become America's favorite mid-size car. This year we've added

improved pollution controls and a long lasting generator, among other things. Improvements with a purpose. We want your 1972 Chevelle to be the best car you ever owned. It's our way of building a better way to see the U.S.A.

Chevrolet

20

21

22

24

23

Vol. XX.   FEBRUARY—MARCH, 1899.   No.

Life insurance companies, such as the Union Mutual in Portland, frequently adopted a lighthouse as their corporate logo because it suggested that their policy could help a family weather the storms, illnesses, or accidents they were likely to encounter during the normal course of life.

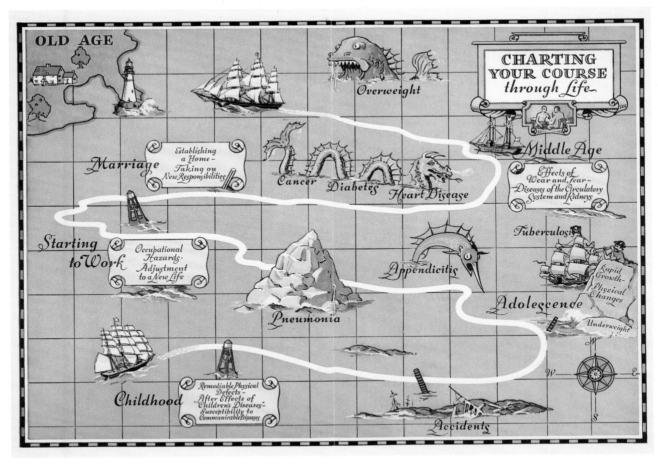

25

But by far the longest and most successful commercial use of the Portland Head Light, or of any other American lighthouse for that matter, was its employment as a logo by the Union Mutual Life Insurance Company. Incorporated in Maine in 1848, Union Mutual moved its headquarters from Boston to Portland in 1881, and in the mid-1890s it began to use Portland Head as its symbol on stationery, policies, and insurance checks, although the light was not officially adopted as the company's logo until 1941. Promotional materials produced by the firm prior to the introduction of Portland Head had been mostly giveaways for agents to distribute, useful items such as calendars, blotters, and household guides aimed at women, but none of them bore any trademark that could be associated with the company. Poems were sometimes distributed, such as an illustrated c. 1890 edition of Gray's *Elegy Written in a Country Churchyard* (left above), but its "implications of mortality for the in-dividual readers"[1] were subsequently deemed to be a bit lugubrious. A more positive symbol of the company was needed. Hence, the introduction of the Portland Head Light shortly thereafter as an identifying device on both giveaways and company publications was welcomed because "the old lighthouse on its solid rock foundation" would be "associated in the public mind with the reliability of the Union Mutual."[2] A more literal interpretation would seem to suggest that the company was ready to help any family to survive the storm that drowned its breadwinner. In any case, Union Mutual continued to employ the Portland Head Light or an abstracted version of a lighthouse as its logo for more than a hundred years, even after the company was taken public in 1986 and renamed UNUM Corporation. The lighthouse was finally relinquished as a corporate emblem in 1998 when the firm was merged with the Provident Companies.

26

27

28
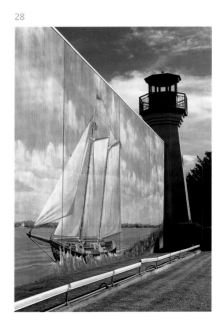

29

30

If you drive down Route 1 anywhere along the coast, you will inevitably encounter lighthouse replicas large and small, standing and sometimes flashing as signposts for roadside businesses, usually restaurants, alehouses, motels, gift shops, miniature golf courses, or realtors. The association between tower and the service or product being touted is sometimes reasonable—lobstermen haul traps near lighthouses (think seafood restaurant) and weekend sailors need lighthouses to keep them afloat in the boats they buy (think boat dealership). Sometimes the connection is imaginative—a lighthouse seems appropriate on a miniature golf course that features vestigial versions of Maine's most iconic buildings and topographical features. And occasionally the relationship is nonexistent—what does a ten-foot lighthouse painted with cows have to do with the parking lot it tries to attract you to in Boothbay Harbor? Regardless of the association, however, fake highway lighthouses always do what they are supposed to do: their distinctive shape catches your eye as you drive by and causes you to glimpse what's being offered.

It's hard to miss the landlocked lights and signboard beacons that compete for your attention as you drive along Maine's coastal highways. (Figs. 32–38)

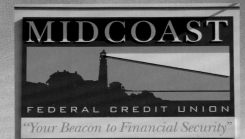

39

40

41

42

43

Individual souvenirs like these have long been available, but entrepreneurs in Maine helped to develop a new fad in the 1990s for decorating home interiors with a lighthouse theme by introducing a broad range of household products, either shaped like a light tower or adorned with lighthouse images.

You may have noticed recently that more and more small lighthouse replicas have been sprouting from people's lawns as lampposts, birdhouses, and garden ornaments. And you might have seen them appearing inside homes as well, cleverly adapted to serve as chandeliers, side tables, candlesticks, Christmas ornaments, or some such. Over the course of the last twenty years, almost any common household item you can think of, whether decorative or utilitarian, has been given a tapered cylindrical form with a lantern on top or decorated with lighthouses on its surface and offered for sale. Such a vast range of practical items and decorative accessories is now available that anyone who loves those lonely beacons can completely furnish, equip, and decorate any space at home with lighthouse paraphernalia, from living room and kitchen to bedroom and bathroom.

This kind of marketing is the contemporary extension of another great Maine tradition: "If you can get them to come to Maine for a visit, be sure to sell them something they can remember it by." Travel souvenirs are not a Maine invention, of course, since people have been seeking and collecting mementos of their tours and pilgrimages since the seventeenth century. Inexpensive trinkets bearing the image of local landmarks are available worldwide and are all too familiar: spoons, key chains, magnets, thimbles, pens, and whatnot. What is different now in Maine is that so many of the lighthouse-related gifts that are being offered are more practical and diverse in nature and better made, durable items intended for use in the home rather than throwaways. In addition, the new lines of collectibles that have been created are of higher quality, especially the models of individual lighthouses.

THE SOUTHERN MAINE

Coastal Beacon

A FREE WEEKLY REGIONAL NEWSPAPER

Published every Thursday   Southern Maine's regional weekly magazine   August 18 • August 25, 1994   Volume II, Issue 33

Lighthouse Month
Lighthouse Mania

When you've got a good idea, it's only a matter of time before the public catches on... then you've got to ride the whirlwind.

Kathy Finnegan and Tim Harrison of Lighthouse Gifts, who opened their gift shop in Wells last May, specializing in lighthouse collectibles, lighthouse books and videos, lighthouse T-shirts and belt buckles, and (you guessed it) all kinds of other lighthouse **stuff**, are on the verge of an explosion.

"We haven't had a bad day since April," says Tim, while their parking lot is full of cars with out-of-state plates (with plenty of Maine ones too). And so, at a time when they can't keep up with the demand for lighthouse memorabilia at their shop, while they are hiring new people to help cope with the demand, and while they

already don't have enough parking spots for eager shoppers, Kathy and Tim just naturally thought it was time to take on some new projects... including taking Lighthouse Gifts nationwide.

This week has seen the completion of "Lighthouse Depot," the world's first catalog devoted exclusively to lighthouse collectibles. Billed as "The most complete selection of Lighthouse memorabilia ever assembled," the catalog lists hundreds of items throughout its packed, full color forty eight pages.

To put the catalog together, they not only had to hire photographers, models, and design the catalog, they also had to assemble a mailing list of 125,000 people, set up a 24-hour telephone bank, a computer network, a whole new telephone system, and find warehousing space in an already crowded building. And that was just the start.

From start to finish, it was a complex and expensive project, requiring thousands of man-hours to complete.

All this on top of running an already

houses.

Kathy Finnegan started it with Tim se... years ago when the... moved to Maine an... visited every lighthouse in the state, says "W... anticipate out-growing our building within a year." The extra space ... required for the telephone operators and the shipping system needed for the catalog sales has already crowded the ... farmhouse which hol... Lighthouse Gifts to ... limits. And the fact ... the store itself alrea... needs to expand to ke... up with current demand place an enormous strain on their available resources. Currently, they have used up almost every square foot in the building, and have truc... containers in the back yard to provide additional storage space.

And it ... pened in le... a year and ... Kathy s... hope for a good return

A brand new Ki...
Page...

with local events, ... and much mo...

See page 10...

LIGHTHOUSE DEPOT

Gifts

COLLECTIBLES
SOUVENIRS
CLOTHING
VIDEOS
JEWELERY
BOOKS

THE WORLD'S LARGEST LIGHTHOUSE STORE

ENTRANCE 75 FT.

Going Places

Tim and Kathy are surrounded by some of their 7,000 or more lighthouses.

A Love of Lighthouses

IN 1989 KATHY FINNEGAN AND Tim Harrison came east from Chicago and set out to see the lighthouses of Maine. "It wasn't until we got started," Tim recalls, "that we realized Maine has 68 lighthouses. And Kathy wanted to touch every single one."

The more lighthouses they visited, the more they wanted to learn. "Someone ought to write a book," Tim said. So they did, followed by a monthly newspaper, *Lighthouse Digest*, and then a small mail order business selling lighthouse souvenirs. When the couple found they were devoting too much time to tracking down the hundreds of companies that made lighthouse products, they decided to open a store to house them all—Lighthouse Gifts in Wells.

"There's no other place like it," Kathy says. "We know, because we spent years looking for one."

Tim and Kathy stock over 7,000 lighthouse items from both coasts, the Great Lakes, Canada's Maritimes, and overseas. The gifts range from 99¢ trinkets to handsome collectibles such as the Harbor Lights series of lighthouse replicas, each signed and numbered.

"This isn't a place where you'll find many generic lighthouses," adds Tim. "We're here to educate. Almost everything we stock is a replica of a real lighthouse."

A tourist trap this is not. Part curators and part merchants, Tim and Kathy are inventing this unique

photograph by Doug Mindell

No one is more responsible for promoting the mania for lighthouse-inspired furnishings and paraphernalia than Tim Harrison and Kathleen Finnegan, who opened Lighthouse Depot on Route 1 in Wells in 1993 with seven thousand items in stock.

How this development came about is an important story in itself, reflective not only of the entrepreneurship that Maine seems to engender but also of the growing interest in the history and preservation of the state's lighthouses. Much of the credit for shifting the gift business in this more practical and historical direction should go to the couple who founded Lighthouse Depot in Wells, Tim Harrison and Kathleen Finnegan.

When Tim and Kathleen first came to Maine on vacation in 1989, they became so fascinated with its lighthouses that they ended up moving to the state from Chicago, renting a caravan, and camping out for six months in order to explore and photograph each of the sixty-six light stations. The outcome of this adventure was a ninety-six-page color guidebook, *Lighthouses of Maine and New Hampshire*, self-published in 1991 and successfully self-distributed in a total of thirty thousand copies. Typical of all their future business ventures, the emphasis was on the historical appreciation and preservation of the lighthouses, as stated in the book's introduction: "Through the pages of this publication, it is our dream that you too may become a lighthouse enthusiast and by joining any one of the various lighthouse organizations, you will help in the preservation of a little slice of our American History."[3]

Worried about the future of the lighthouses because the Coast Guard was either automating the towers or vacating entire stations, Tim and Kathleen's next endeavor was to start a magazine that would provide news about what was happening to the lighthouses, articles exploring their history, and a list of the most endangered beacons. Launched on a shoestring in May 1992, *Lighthouse Digest* now reaches twenty-three thousand subscribers in all fifty states and seventeen other countries.

In their initial exploration of the lighthouse scene in Maine, Tim and Kathleen had also noticed that there were surprisingly few lighthouse products available in gift stores. Having learned from the sales of their guide-book how many lighthouse buffs were out there looking for gifts and collectibles that would reflect their interest, and having realized that sales of well-made mementos were useful to local organizations trying to raise money for lighthouse museums and restoration projects, they decided that their next venture would be to establish a store that sold only lighthouse-themed goods. The Lighthouse Depot, "the world's largest lighthouse gift store," opened in May 1993, with a stock of over seven thousand lighthouse items made in America, Canada, and overseas. After *Yankee* magazine published an article on the store in its August 1994 issue, "A tourist trap this is not,"[4] and after Don Devine joined the firm to initiate catalogue sales, goods moved out the door at a rapid pace, especially the accurately detailed, intricately sculpted, hand-painted models of individual lighthouses.

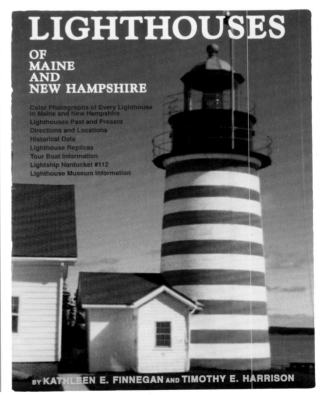

LIGHTHOUSES
OF MAINE AND NEW HAMPSHIRE

Color Photographs of Every Lighthouse in Maine and New Hampshire
Lighthouses Past and Present
Directions and Locations
Historical Data
Lighthouse Replicas
Tour Boat Information
Lightship Nantucket #112
Lighthouse Museum Information

BY KATHLEEN E. FINNEGAN AND TIMOTHY E. HARRISON

53

Needless to say, other gift stores in Maine and across the country took note. Lighthouse Depot had started the trend that led manufacturers to make and retailers to sell all of the items necessary for creating romantic lighthouse-themed interiors within the home, a fad that would give new meaning to the old saying: "We'll keep the light on for you."

Businesses that profit from the existence of lighthouses have sometimes been criticized for diverting funds that are needed for the upkeep and preservation of the lights or condemned for diminishing their significance with cheap imitations. That has not been the case in Maine. The logos that feature the lighthouses, the ads and websites that emphasize their history, and the funny roadside structures that mimic them, all these have contributed to greater public appreciation of the light stations at a crucial point in their history when so many of them have been vacated because of automation. Higher quality collectibles, especially architectural models and fine posters, have also helped to spur new interest in the beauty and variety of lighthouses and increase awareness of the need to rescue and maintain endangered beacons. Sales of such items have also been a good source of revenue for lighthouse preservation societies and museums, so that when you're in Maine and read a slogan like "Saving Lighthouses, One Gift at a Time,"[5] you have to take it seriously.

A Maine catalogue offers models of lighthouses from all over the United States, displaying their variety and tempting the customer to begin collecting them.

55

Alan Claude. *Portland Head Light, Cumberland County, Maine.*
© Alan Claude 2007.

This photograph of the Egg Rock Light Station in 1991 illustrates what often happened during the Coast Guard's automation program: windows and doors were boarded up, maintenance was deferred, and the grounds became unkempt. Consequences such as these spurred the public to take action to properly preserve the lighthouses, beginning in the 1980s.

Saving the Sentinels

The Preservation of Maine's Light Stations

Kirk F. Mohney

2

Unlike the early forts and meeting houses that Maine citizens rallied around in the nineteenth and early twentieth centuries to save from demolition or deterioration, lighthouses became the subject of concerted public preservation efforts only in the last three decades. As long as the federal government was still using and maintaining lighthouses as it had historically, there was little cause to be concerned about their disappearance. However, as the Coast Guard's program to automate the lights and remove the keepers from the stations neared its completion in the 1980s, public concern for the preservation of these distinctive historic properties intensified.

The earliest known public action to preserve lighthouses in Maine dates to the 1930s, when the federal government discontinued a number of light stations and disposed of the lighthouses and their associated build-ings. Among the properties sold in this period, Grindel Point and Dice Head were acquired by the towns of Islesboro and Castine, respectively. In 1940, the town of Bristol negotiated with the federal government to purchase the land and all buildings—except the lighthouse—at Pemaquid Point for the purpose of establishing a public park. All these initial public and private purchasers preserved the lighthouses and keepers' houses, as well as many of the outbuildings, setting an example of stewardship that has been followed by every subsequent new owner of a Maine light station.

When the Coast Guard assumed responsibility for the nation's light stations in 1939, it inherited an automation program that had commenced in Maine in 1934 when six lighthouses were converted to automatic acetylene gas or electric operation. Although the Coast Guard also automated the Lubec Channel Light in 1939, the program

3   4   5

did not get underway in earnest until the 1950s. Between 1954 and 1983, more than thirty additional lighthouses in Maine were automated. While the towers and fog signals that remained in use were maintained, the keepers' houses and other buildings were boarded up or demolished, sometimes in spectacular fashion as when Special Forces teams destroyed buildings at Two Bush Island and Moose Peak in the early 1970s and 1980s. Notable preservation efforts were made in this period, however. For example, the Monhegan Associates, Inc., acquired the remaining outbuildings at the Monhegan Island Light Station in 1962 and opened the Monhegan Museum to the public six years later. In 1973, the College of the Atlantic entered into a lease agreement with the Coast Guard to use and maintain the keeper's house on Mount Desert Rock as a research and education field station.

Concern for the future of the historic artifacts that were being removed from the lighthouses as a result of the modernization and automation process led Ken Black, a chief warrant officer in the Coast Guard, to begin to collect and preserve them in the 1960s. Among the items saved were examples of the glass Fresnel lenses that had been installed in Maine lighthouses beginning in the 1850s. To raise public awareness about the history of light stations and the challenges involved in preserving their buildings and equipment, Black founded the Shore Village Museum in Rockland in 1978 and began publishing a newsletter about lighthouse-related happenings in Maine and around the country. His collection of artifacts subsequently became the core of today's Maine Lighthouse Museum when it was established in Rockland in 2005.

Several events in the 1980s helped to heighten public appreciation of the preservation issues confronting Maine's historic lighthouses. In 1985, Maine Citizens for Historic Preservation (now Maine Preservation) spon-

sored a conference titled "Maine's Lighthouses: Preservation Challenges and Solutions" that brought together individuals with an interest and expertise in lighthouses as well as governmental and private nonprofit entities. The conference highlighted the growing interest in lighthouses not only in Maine but in the rest of the nation as well. That same year, the Maine Historic Preservation Commission initiated a two-year documentation project that resulted in listing thirty-eight lighthouses in the National Register of Historic Places. In 1987, the Island Institute (founded in 1983 as a conservation organization to support Maine's island communities) published *Keeping the Light: A Handbook for Adaptive Re-Use of Island Lighthouse Stations* to assist municipalities and private groups in preparing and managing unmanned lighthouses and their outbuildings for new uses. Then, late the same year, Congress passed a bill sponsored by Maine Senator George Mitchell to create the Bicentennial Lighthouse Fund for the purpose of funding lighthouse preservation. On the basis of the number of its lighthouses listed in the National Register, Maine received $350,000 from the fund over a three-year period to support the work of governmental and nonprofit organizations working to preserve lighthouse properties.

6

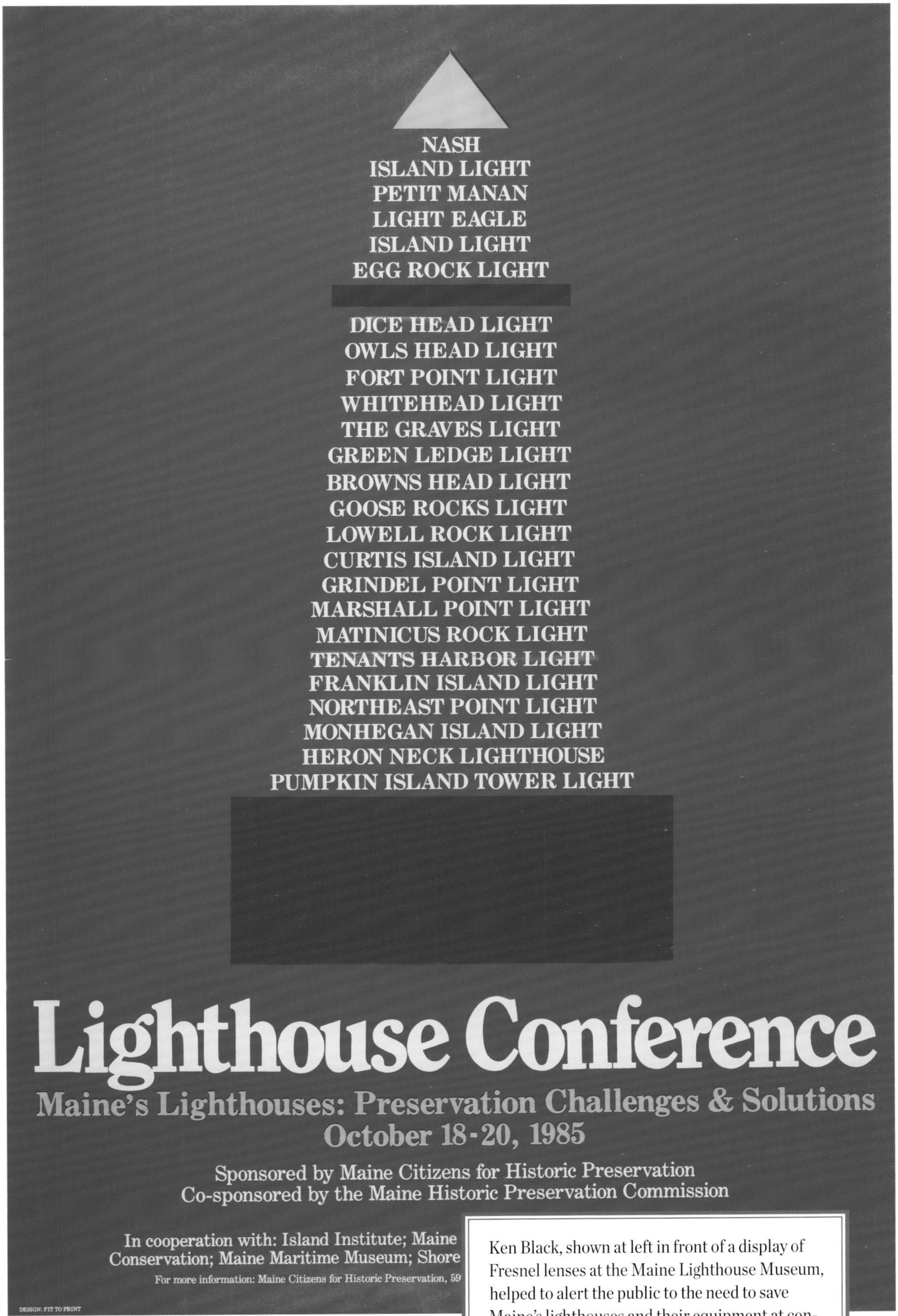

NASH
ISLAND LIGHT
PETIT MANAN
LIGHT EAGLE
ISLAND LIGHT
EGG ROCK LIGHT

DICE HEAD LIGHT
OWLS HEAD LIGHT
FORT POINT LIGHT
WHITEHEAD LIGHT
THE GRAVES LIGHT
GREEN LEDGE LIGHT
BROWNS HEAD LIGHT
GOOSE ROCKS LIGHT
LOWELL ROCK LIGHT
CURTIS ISLAND LIGHT
GRINDEL POINT LIGHT
MARSHALL POINT LIGHT
MATINICUS ROCK LIGHT
TENANTS HARBOR LIGHT
FRANKLIN ISLAND LIGHT
NORTHEAST POINT LIGHT
MONHEGAN ISLAND LIGHT
HERON NECK LIGHTHOUSE
PUMPKIN ISLAND TOWER LIGHT

Lighthouse Conference

Maine's Lighthouses: Preservation Challenges & Solutions
October 18-20, 1985

Sponsored by Maine Citizens for Historic Preservation
Co-sponsored by the Maine Historic Preservation Commission

In cooperation with: Island Institute; Maine
Conservation; Maine Maritime Museum; Shore
For more information: Maine Citizens for Historic Preservation, 59

DESIGN: FIT TO PRINT

Ken Black, shown at left in front of a display of
Fresnel lenses at the Maine Lighthouse Museum,
helped to alert the public to the need to save
Maine's lighthouses and their equipment at con-
ferences such as the one advertised here.

At one time, the Libby Island Light Station featured a keeper's house, an assistant keeper's house, a boathouse, and a rain shed, in addition to the extant granite lighthouse and brick fog signal building shown here. Wooden buildings are particularly susceptible to rapid deterioration in Maine's harsh marine environment, as is evident in the inset photographs of the boathouse at Petit Manan (no longer extant) and the bell house at Perkins Island (restored). (Figs. 8–10)

11

Nationally, two nonprofit organizations devoted to the preservation of lighthouses and the study of their history were founded in 1984: the United States Lighthouse Society in Washington State and the Lighthouse Preservation Society in Massachusetts. On the federal level, the Coast Guard, the Advisory Council on Historic Preservation, and the National Conference of State Historic Preservation Officers reached an agreement to begin leasing the stations, an action that addressed the problem of how to maintain the outbuildings no longer needed after the automation of the towers.

An important test of the private nonprofit sector's ability to preserve Maine's lighthouses began on April 19, 1989, when a fire at Heron Neck Light Station substantially damaged the keeper's house. After the Coast Guard announced plans to demolish what remained of the building, the Island Institute stepped forward with a proposal to gain title to the property rather than lease it so that the keeper's house could be restored. Since the Coast Guard was planning to dispose of seven more light stations in Maine in the early 1990s, these negotiations with the Island Institute helped to persuade it to shift away from the policy of leasing or licensing lighthouses to one that emphasized outright transfer. An agreement for the transfer of Heron Neck Light Station was finally reached in 1993 and was authorized by Congress later that year (along with the transfer of three other light-

houses, including Portland Head Light Station to the town of Cape Elizabeth and Burnt Coat Harbor Light Station to the town of Swan's Island). The Island Institute later leased Heron Neck to a private individual who reconstructed the fire-damaged dwelling.

Based on the success of the Heron Neck Light Station transfer and the Coast Guard's continuing interest in disposing of its lighthouse properties, Peter Ralston at the Island Institute initiated discussions in 1994 with Ted Dernago in the Coast Guard's Real Property Office at the Civil Engineering Unit in Providence, Rhode Island, about a concept for expediting the transfer of Maine's light stations to governmental agencies or nonprofit entities for the purpose of preserving them in perpetuity. These negotiations led to legislation that was introduced in the One hundred and third Congress by Senator Mitchell and brought to passage by Senator Olympia Snowe in 1996 to authorize the transfer of thirty-five lights and one fog signal station in Maine (including four direct transfers to the U. S. Fish and Wildlife Service) through a process that came to be known as the Maine Lights Program. As a result of this program, twenty-four lighthouses were subsequently transferred to nonprofit organizations, educational institutions, municipalities, and the state, thereby initiating a new era of lighthouse preservation in Maine.

12

URIER-GAZETTE

SINCE 1846

The Courier-Gazette
USPS 135-700
Rockland, Maine 04841
Second Class Postage Paid

unty, surrounding towns and the islands of Penobscot Bay three times a week.

day-Saturday   TWENTY PAGES — 45¢ COPY   Volume 144, Number 50

Heron Neck Light Burns

by Steve Heddericg
News Editor

VINALHAVEN — A state fire marshal was on his way to Greens Island Monday afternoon to determine the cause of an Saturday morning blaze that heavily damaged Heron Neck Light Station.

Vinalhaven Fire Chief Cy Davidson said Monday he was "almost certain the cause was electrical," but was awaiting Fire Marshal Steve Dixon's determination.

Davidson said smoke was reported coming from the 135-year-old light station at about 7 a.m. Saturday by fisherman Ronnie Peterson. The station sits high on a rocky bluff at the southern tip of Greens Island, about two miles from Carver's Harbor on Vinalhaven.

Two boats rushed 25 island firefighters to the light station, arriving as white smoke billowed out from the eaves of the building. The round, brick light tower is attached to the keeper's house, and was not touched in the blaze. According to Coast Guard officials, the light tower is protected with heat-sensitive Halon fire extinguishers, but the keeper's house was not.

The tower was established in 1854, acco Village Mu Ken Black. house was e and an oil ho 1903.

It named Register of H January 1988

The station boarded up automated

13

COMPLIMENTARY ISSUE   MAY 1992

Massachusetts Developer to Save Historic Light Station

One of the biggest uproars in lighthouse preservation history is drawing to a close with the Coast Guard's announcement that it has picked a lessee for historic and fire damaged Heron Neck Light Station.

In what gained national attention from nearly every newspaper in the United States and the NBC Today Show, a nearly 2 year bureaucratic nightmare will come to a close and a new happier beginning for everyone concerned.

It has been nearly 3 years since an electrical fire destroyed part of the keeper's quarters at Heron Neck Lighthouse which sits majestically atop a cliff of sand colored granite on Greens Island southwest of Carvers Harbor near Vinalhaven Maine.

Heron Neck, built in 1854 and on the National List of Historic Places, is a picture perfect post card location, except for the gaping hole in the roof caused by the fire which has left the building exposed to the elements and deterioration.

The Coast Guard, which is not in the business of maintaining obsolete structures, had assembled a demolition crew to tear down the damaged

HERON NECK RESCUE

reprieve. The Coast Guard agreed that it would lease the buildings out, but it took over 2 years of red tape to finally decide who would actually be awarded the lease.

The lease has been awarded to

restoration having restored a 95 year old lifesaving station in Damariscove Island Maine.

Peter Ralston of the Island Institute in Rockland Maine who was instrumental in saving Heron Neck from quoted as saying

on page 2

The sequence of illustrations beginning on the opposite page shows the Heron Neck Light Station prior to 1896 when the original keeper's house was replaced, during and immediately after the 1989 fire, and in its current condition with the reconstructed dwelling.

16

17

18

The work of preserving Maine's lighthouses has required the dedicated effort of many individuals and organizations, and has ranged in complexity from the relatively straightforward task of re-shingling a bell house to the intricate process of restoring a first order Fresnel lens.

19

20

21

22

The Maine Lights Program was a pioneering effort that assisted the Coast Guard through a state-level process in disposing of a large group of lighthouses by identifying those organizations and governmental agencies that were capable of and committed to preserving them. The Maine Historic Preservation Commission works closely with the new owners of lighthouses transferred during the program to assist them in achieving their goals and expectations.

Subsequent transfers of lighthouses in Maine, and throughout the nation, are now governed by the provisions of the National Historic Lighthouse Preservation Act of 2000 (NHLPA). The Little River Light Station was the first Maine lighthouse to be transferred under the NHLPA. It was deeded to the American Lighthouse Foundation (ALF), successor to the New England Lighthouse Foundation, a nonprofit organization founded in Maine in 1994 by Tim Harrison. Several lighthouses that have not yet been processed through the provisions of the NHLPA have been licensed to ALF, and are being preserved through its efforts.

With the exception of a handful of lighthouses that currently remain in the sole custody of the Coast Guard, the responsibility for preserving Maine's light stations now lies with a diverse group of nonprofit organizations, educational institutions, governmental agencies, and private entities. Their efforts to preserve, restore, and adapt these historic properties for new uses have been admirable. After the uncertainty of the 1980s and 1990s, the future for Maine's lighthouses appears bright.

Sunrise over Frenchman Bay with Egg Rock Light Station in the foreground. Volunteers help to maintain the exterior of the lighthouse which is now owned by the U. S. Fish and Wildlife Service.

23

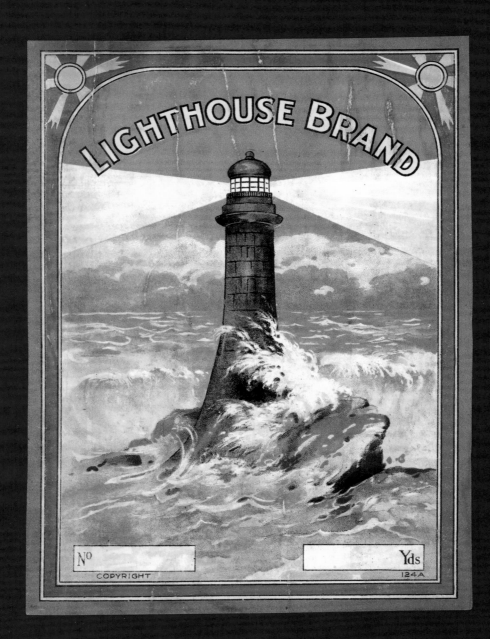

About the Contributors

W. H. BUNTING is a sailor, farmer, digger of ponds, and the author of *Portrait of a Port: Boston 1852–1914; Steamers, Schooners, Cutters and Sloops; A Day's Work,* in two volumes; *Sea Struck; Live Yankees: The Sewalls and Their Ships;* with Earle G. Shettleworth, Jr., *An Eye for the Coast;* and *The Camera's Coast: Historic Images of Sea and Shore in New England.* He lives in Whitefield, Maine.

RICHARD CHEEK is a collector of American design books and graphic ephemera who helped to found Historic New England's visual history series and serves as its editor. As an architectural and landscape photographer, he is the author of fifteen books, including *Land of the Commonwealth: A Portrait of the Conserved Landscapes of Massachusetts* and *Mount Auburn Cemetery: Beauty on the Edge of Eternity.*

THOMAS ANDREW DENENBERG is the director of Shelburne Museum, Shelburne, Vermont. A graduate of Bates College, he earned a doctorate from Boston University and has written extensively on the image of New England.

TIMOTHY HARRISON is the publisher and editor of *Lighthouse Digest,* a Maine-based lighthouse news and history magazine, and he is the cofounder and past president of the American Lighthouse Foundation. In 2005 he was the recipient of the Department of Homeland Security's United States Coast Guard Public Service Award for his role in saving lighthouses and the history associated with them.

KIRK F. MOHNEY is the assistant director of the Maine Historic Preservation Commission and serves as Maine's deputy state historic preservation officer. He is the author of books about Maine library and railroad buildings, and he wrote the National Register of Historic Places Multiple Property Documentation Form for lighthouses in Maine.

DAVID RICHARDS is the interim director of the University of Maine Margaret Chase Smith Library in Skowhegan, Maine. He is the author of *Poland Spring: A Tale of the Gilded Age* and a contributor to *A Landscape History of New England.*

EARLE G. SHETTLEWORTH, JR., is the director of the Maine Historic Preservation Commission and serves as Maine's state historian. He is the author or coauthor of many books on Maine architecture, art, and photography, including monographs on Eric Hudson and S. P. R. Triscott, Monhegan Island artists and photographers who created memorable maritime images with paint brush and camera.

SENATOR OLYMPIA J. SNOWE of Maine was elected to the United States Senate in 1994 and is presently serving her third term. She has been a champion for the preservation of the state's lighthouses, having brought to passage the legislation that established the Maine Lights Program.

Illustration Sources, Endnotes, and Bibliography

LIGHTHOUSE NAMES

Almost all Maine lighthouses are named for their geographic location. During the nineteenth century, as the federal government gradually developed an overlapping system of lighthouses along the state's coast, the number of support buildings surrounding each tower increased to typically include a keeper's house, a boathouse, a fog bell house, and an oil house, if not additional structures. In the *Light List,* which the Light House Board began to issue annually in the 1850s, this complex of buildings was referred to as a *light station.* Thus a lighthouse and its outbuildings, like those at Portland Head on Cape Elizabeth, would be listed as Portland Head Light Station.

In the 1930s, once the lighthouses began to be automated and the keepers dismissed, only the tower and fog signal building at converted stations needed to be maintained, which made any other buildings on site superfluous. As the project to automate all Maine's lights neared completion, the Coast Guard dropped the term *station* from its *Light List,* reflecting the shift to unmanned lighthouses. This abbreviated form, e.g., Portland Head Light, has since become the most popular way to refer to each lighthouse, regardless of the number of surviving outbuildings.

In keeping with the current *Light List,* this book uses the word *Light* as part of the proper name of individual lighthouses except in the architecture chapter, which covers the period when the light stations were being constructed and fully utilized, and the preservation chapter, which describes the efforts to save the stations' outbuildings after the towers were automated. When a possessive apostrophe appears in a name, it reflects period usage.

Opening Illustrations

PAGE 1: Cape Elizabeth Light, northeast tower seen from southwest tower, Cape Elizabeth, 1989. Richard Cheek, photographer.
FRONTISPIECE: Light tower and Fresnel lens, Cape Elizabeth Light, Cape Elizabeth, 1989. Richard Cheek, photographer.
TITLE PAGE: Goat Island Light doorstop, mid-twentieth century. Justin Goodstein-Aue, photographer. Promised gift to Historic New England.
PAGE 4: Hassan tobacco cards depicting Boon Island Light, Matinicus Rock Light, Goat Island Light, and Owl's Head Light, 1912. Verso of Owl's Head Light card. G. W. Gail & Ax's tobacco card depicting Vineyard Sound Lightship, late nineteenth century. Promised gift to Historic New England.
PAGE 6: Cover for the *Saturday Evening Post,* September 22, 1945, by Stevan Dohanos. Illustration © SEPS licensed by Curtis Licensing, Indianapolis, Indiana. All rights reserved. *Lighthouse Digest* archives.

Introduction

ENDNOTE
1. "The Lighthouse," by Henry Wadsworth Longfellow, from *The Seaside and the Fireside.* (Boston: Ticknor, Reed, and Fields, 1850), 41–44.

> The rocky ledge runs far into the sea,
>   And on its outer point, some miles away,
> The Lighthouse lifts its massive masonry,
>   A pillar of fire by night, of cloud by day.
>
> Even at this distance I can see the tides,
>   Upheaving, break unheard along its base,
> A speechless wrath, that rises and subsides
>   In the white lip and tremor of the face.

And as the evening darkens, lo! how bright,
  Through the deep purple of the twilight air,
Beams forth the sudden radiance of its light
  With strange, unearthly splendor in its glare!

Not one alone; from each projecting cape
  And perilous reef along the ocean's verge,
Starts into life a dim, gigantic shape,
  Holding its lantern o'er the restless surge.

Like the great giant Christopher it stands
  Upon the brink of the tempestuous wave,
Wading far out among the rocks and sands,
  The night-o'ertaken mariner to save.

And the great ships sail outward and return,
  Bending and bowing o'er the billowy swells,
And ever joyful, as they see it burn,
  They wave their silent welcomes and farewells.

They come forth from the darkness, and their sails
  Gleam for a moment only in the blaze,
And eager faces, as the light unveils,
  Gaze at the tower, and vanish while they gaze.

The mariner remembers when a child,
  On his first voyage, he saw it fade and sink;
And when, returning from adventures wild,
  He saw it rise again o'er ocean's brink.

Steadfast, serene, immovable, the same
  Year after year, through all the silent night
Burns on for evermore that quenchless flame,
  Shines on that inextinguishable light!

It sees the ocean to its bosom clasp
  The rocks and sea-sand with the kiss of peace;
It sees the wild winds lift it in their grasp,
  And hold it up, and shake it like a fleece.

The startled waves leap over it; the storm
  Smites it with all the scourges of the rain,
And steadily against its solid form
  Press the great shoulders of the hurricane.

The sea-bird wheeling round it, with the din
  Of wings and winds and solitary cries,
Blinded and maddened by the light within,
  Dashes himself against the glare, and dies.

A new Prometheus, chained upon the rock,
  Still grasping in his hand the fire of Jove,
It does not hear the cry, nor heed the shock,
  But hails the mariner with words of love.

"Sail on!" it says, "sail on, ye stately ships!
  And with your floating bridge the ocean span;
Be mine to guard this light from all eclipse,
  Be yours to bring man nearer unto man!"

Throw Out the Lifeline!
Wrecks and the Hazards of Coastal Navigation

ILLUSTRATION SOURCES

1. Sheet music cover for "The Hurricane," 1906. By S. L. Alpert and arranged by E. T. Paull. A. Hoen and Company, lithographers. E. T. Paull Music Company, publisher. Promised gift to Historic New England.

2. "Wreck of the 'Bohemian' as seen the Morning after She Sunk," from *Harper's Weekly*, March 12, 1864. Promised gift to Historic New England.

3. Nathaniel Currier (American, 1813–1888). *Awful Conflagration of the Steam Boat* Lexington, undated. Hand-colored lithograph. 8⅜ × 12⅛ in. Gift of Lenore B. and Sidney A. Alpert, supplemented with Museum Acquisition Funds. Michele and Donald D'Amour Museum of Fine Arts, Springfield, Massachusetts. David Stansbury, photographer. This lithograph was first published in 1840.

4. "The Wreck of the 'Schiller'—Bishop's Rock Light," from *Harper's Weekly*, May 29, 1875. J. O. Davidson, illustrator. Promised gift to Historic New England.

5. Newspaper clipping reporting the loss of the steamer *Narragansett*, from the *Boston Journal*, June 12, 1880. Promised gift to Historic New England.

6. Newspaper clipping reporting the collision of the steamers *Narragansett* and *Stonington*, from the *Boston Journal*, June 12, 1880. Promised gift to Historic New England.

7. "A Story of the Sea, Incidents in the Life of a Sailor," from *Harper's Weekly*, March 12, 1864. Promised gift to Historic New England.

8. "The Fisherman's Children," from *Sea Pictures Drawn with Pen and Pencil* by James Macaulay. (London: Religious Tract Society, c. 1880.) Private collection.

9. Program cover from an event for the Society for the Relief of Destitute Children of Seamen, July 20, 1904. Promised gift to Historic New England.

10. Gravestone of Captains Allen Hodgdon and Granvill Hodgdon, Boothbay (1857), 2010. Richard Cheek, photographer.

11. Gravestone of Alevia Hodgdon, wife of Captain A. K. Hodgdon, Boothbay (1872), 2010. Richard Cheek, photographer.

12. Frontispiece from *Episodes of the Sea in Former Days: A Book for Boys.* (London: Blackie and Sons, 1880.) Private collection.

13. Winslow Homer (American, 1836–1910). *The Fog Warning.* 1885. Oil on canvas. 30¼ × 48½ in. Museum of Fine Arts, Boston. Otis Norcross Fund, 94.72. Photograph © 2012 Museum of Fine Arts, Boston.

14. Schooners in fog off Cape Elizabeth, c. 1904. Photographer unknown. Courtesy of Jean M. Deighan.

15. "Operation of a Siren (Steam Fog-Horn)—Sectional View" in "The Lighthouses of the United States" by Charles Nordhoff, from *Harper's Magazine,* March 1874. Historic New England Library and Archives.

16. Map from an Eastern Steamship Lines brochure, 1930. Promised gift to Historic New England.

17. Cover of a map and timetable for the Casco Bay and Harpswell Lines, 1911. Promised gift to Historic New England.

18. The steamship *City of Bangor*, 1906. Nathaniel L. Stebbins, photographer. Historic New England Library and Archives.

19. The steamship *City of Bangor* grounded, 1902. Photographer unknown. Maine State Museum.

20. "The Wreck of the 'Atlantic'—Cast Up By the Sea," from *Harper's Weekly*, April 26, 1873. Winslow Homer, illustrator. Promised gift to Historic New England.

21. "Driven to the North in the Hurricane of 1703," from *Sea Pictures Drawn with Pen and Pencil* by James Macaulay. (London: Religious Tract Society, c. 1880.) Private collection.

22. Illustration from *The Wreck of the Hesperus* by Henry Wadsworth Longfellow. (New York: E. P. Dutton and Company, 1888.)

23. Woodcut from "The Wreck of the Hesperus," from *The Poems of Henry Wadsworth Longfellow*, selected and edited by Louis Untermeyer. Boyd Hanna, engraver. (New York: The Heritage Press, 1943.) Reproduced with the permission of MBI, Inc. Private collection.

24. "The Abandoned," based on a painting by Clarkson Stanfield, from *Sea Pictures Drawn with Pen and Pencil* by James Macaulay. Edmund Evans, engraver. (London: Religious Tract Society, c. 1880.) Private collection.

25. Sheet music cover for "The Ship that Never Returned," 1884. Song by Henry C. Work. W. J. Morgan and Company, lithographer. S. Brainard's Sons, publisher. Lester S. Levy Collection of Sheet Music, Department of Rare Books and Manuscripts, Sheridan Libraries, The Johns Hopkins University, http://levysheetmusic.mse.jhu.edu.

26. Sheet music cover for "Flash Light," 1909. By Edwin Ellis and arranged by E. T. Paull. A. Hoen and Company, lithographers. E. T. Paull Music Company, publisher. Promised gift to Historic New England.

27. Sheet music cover for "The Three Fishers," 1856. Words by Rev. Charles Kingsley and music by S. D. S. and Hullah. P. S. Duval and Son, lithographers. S. T. Gordon, publisher. Lester S. Levy Collection of Sheet Music, Department of Rare Books and Manuscripts, Sheridan Libraries, The Johns Hopkins University, http://levysheetmusic.mse.jhu.edu.

28. Sheet music cover for "The Ship that Sailed from Boston," 1884. Words and music by Charles Eastman. W. J. Morgan and Company, lithographer. S. Brainard's Sons, publisher. Lester S. Levy Collection of Sheet Music, Department of Rare Books and Manuscripts, Sheridan Libraries, The Johns Hopkins University, http://levysheetmusic.mse.jhu.edu.

29. Sheet music cover for "The Storm of Life," 1903. Words by Harry Williams and music by Egbert Vanalstyne. Starmer, illustrator. Shapiro, Bernstein and Company, publisher. Promised gift to Historic New England.

30. Sheet music cover for "The Mariner's Orphan Girl," c. 1845. Words by Thomas Hudson and music by N. J. Sporle. E. W. Bouve, lithographer. Oliver Ditson, publisher. Historic New England Library and Archives.

31. "Historical and Pictorial Map of Casco Bay, Maine," c. 1950. Devised by Edward Rowe Snow and Draper Hill, Jr. Promised gift to Historic New England.

32. Tipped in fragment of wood from the steamer *Portland* and bookplate from the book *New England Sea Tragedies* by Edward Rowe Snow. (New York: Dodd, Mead and Company, 1960.) Promised gift to Historic New England.

33. Cover of *Storms and Shipwrecks of New England* by Edward Rowe Snow. (Boston: Yankee Publishing Company, 1943.) Promised gift to Historic New England.

34. Cover of *True Tales of Terrible Shipwrecks* by Edward Rowe Snow. (New York: Dodd, Mead and Company, 1963.) Promised gift to Historic New England.

35. Cover of *Great Sea Rescues* by Edward Rowe Snow. (New York: Dodd, Mead and Company, 1958.) Promised gift to Historic New England.

36. *The Lighthouse Keeper's Silent Conversation with the Sinking Ship*, by Anne-Emmanuelle Marpeau, 2001. Ben Magro, photographer. Courtesy of Anne-Emmanuelle Marpeau. Cawley Family Collection.

ENDNOTES

1. Benjamin J. Willard, *Captain Ben's Book* (Portland, Maine: Lakeside Press, 1895), 87–93.

2. Willard, *Captain Ben's Book*, 26–27. Presumably he was referring to the White Island grounds, southeast of Boothbay.

3. Charles A. E. Long, *Matinicus Isle, Its Story and Its People* (Lewiston, Maine: Lewiston Journal Print Shop, 1926), 113–18.

4. *The Wreck of the Hesperus* by Henry Wadsworth Longfellow. (New York: E. P. Dutton and Company, 1888.)

The Wreck of the Hesperus

It was the schooner Hesperus
    That sailed the wintry sea;
And the skipper had taken his little daughter
    To bear him company.

Blue were her eyes as the fairy-flax,
    Her cheeks like the dawn of day,
And her bosom white as the hawthorn buds
    That ope in the month of May.

The skipper he stood beside the helm,
    His pipe was in his mouth,
And he watched how the veering flaw did blow
    The smoke now west, now south.

Then up and spake an old sailor,
    Had sailed to the Spanish Main,
"I pray thee, put into yonder port,
    For I fear a hurricane.

"Last night the moon had a golden ring,
    And to-night no moon we see!"
The skipper he blew a whiff from his pipe,
    And a scornful laugh laughed he.

Colder and louder blew the wind,
    A gale from the north-east;
The snow fell hissing in the brine,
    And the billows frothed like yeast.

Down came the storm, and smote amain
    The vessel in its strength;
She shuddered and paused, like a frighted steed,
    Then leaped her cable's length.

"Come hither! come hither, my little daughter,
  And do not tremble so;
For I can weather the roughest gale,
  That ever wind did blow."

He wrapped her warm in his seaman's coat,
  Against the stinging blast;
He cut a rope from a broken spar,
  And bound her to the mast.
"O father! I hear the church-bells ring;
  O say, what may it be?" –
"'Tis a fog-bell on a rock-bound coast!" –
  And he steered for the open sea.

"O father! I hear the sound of guns;
  O say, what may it be?" –
"Some ship in distress, that cannot live
  In such an angry sea!"

"O father! I see a gleaming light;
  O say, what may it be?"
But the father answered never a word, –
  A frozen corpse was he.

Lashed to the helm, all stiff and stark,
  With his face turned to the skies,
The lantern gleamed through the gleaming snow
  On his fixed and glassy eyes.

Then the maiden clasped her hands and prayed
  That savèd she might be;
And she thought of Christ, who stilled the wave,
  On the Lake of Galilee.

And fast through the midnight dark and drear,
  Through the whistling sleet and snow,
Like a sheeted ghost, the vessel swept
  Toward the reef of Norman's Woe.

And ever the fitful gusts between,
  A sound came from the land;
It was the sound of the trampling surf,
  On the rocks and the hard sea-sand.

The breakers were right beneath her bows,
  She drifted a dreary wreck,
And a whooping billow swept the crew
  Like icicles from her deck.

She struck where the white and fleecy waves
  Looked soft as carded wool;
But the cruel rocks, they gored her side
  Like the horns of an angry bull.

Her rattling shrouds, all sheathed in ice,
  With the masts went by the board;
Like a vessel of glass, she strove and sank,
  Ho! ho! the breakers roared.

At daybreak, on the bleak sea-beach,
  A fisherman stood aghast,
To see the form of a maiden fair,
  Lashed close to a drifting mast.

The salt sea was frozen on her breast,
  The salt tears in her eyes;
And he saw her hair, like the brown sea-weed,
  On the billows fall and rise.

Such was the wreck of the Hesperus,
  In the midnight and the snow!
Christ save us all from a death like this,
  On the reef of Norman's Woe!

PRINCIPAL RESOURCES

Knight, Austin M. *Modern Seamanship*. Tenth edition. New York: D. Van Nostrand Company, Inc., 1942.

Patterson, Captain Howard. *Patterson's Illustrated Nautical Encyclopedia*. Cleveland, Ohio: Marine Review Publishing Company, 1901.

Shaping the Towers
The Architecture of the Lighthouses

ILLUSTRATION SOURCES

1. Monhegan Lighthouse #1, 1849, by Alexander Parris. Records of the U. S. Coast Guard, Record Group 26, Lighthouse Plans; Maine. National Archives and Records Administration.

2. Mount Desert Lighthouse #2, 1847, by Alexander Parris. Records of the U. S. Coast Guard, Record Group 26, Lighthouse Plans; Maine. National Archives and Records Administration.

3. Warrant signed by Governor John Hancock and John Avery, Jr., secretary, ordering Alexander Hodgdon, treasurer of the Commonwealth, to pay £150 to Richard Devens, Captain Joseph McLellan, John Fox, and Joseph Noyes, a committee to superintend the construction of a lighthouse at Portland Head, to be used for the construction of a small building for the keeper of the light, February 3, 1790. Maine Historical Society.

4. Entrance wing and light tower, view northeast, Burnt Island Light Station, Pine Cliff, 1991. Richard Cheek, photographer. Library of Congress, Prints and Photographs Division, HABS ME,8–PICLV,1–6.

5. Light tower, Wood Island Light Station, Biddeford Pool, 1991. Richard Cheek, photographer.

6. Supply house, bell tower, and light tower, Pemaquid Point Light Station, Bristol, 1989. Richard Cheek, photographer.

7. Keeper's house, light tower, and whistle house, Portland Head Light Station, Cape Elizabeth, 1992. Richard Cheek, photographer. Library of Congress, Prints and Photographs Division, HABS ME,3–CAPEL,2–20.

8. Whale's Back Lighthouse #3, 1838, by Alexander Parris. Records of the U. S. Coast Guard, Record Group 26, Lighthouse Plans; Maine. National Archives and Records Administration.

9. Portrait of Alexander Parris by W. E. Chickering, c. 1888. The Bostonian Society.

10. "South elevation of the Stone Lighthouse completed upon the Edystone in 1759," from *A Narrative of the Building and a Description of the Construction of the Edystone Lighthouse with Stone* by John Smeaton. (London: G. Nicol, 1793.) Promised gift to Historic New England.

11. Matinicus Lighthouse #4, 1848, by Alexander Parris. Records of the U. S. Coast Guard, Record Group 26, Lighthouse Plans; Maine. National Archives and Records Administration.

12. Saddle Back Ledge Lighthouse #3, 1848, by Alexander Parris. Records of the U. S. Coast Guard, Record Group 26, Lighthouse Plans; Maine. National Archives and Records Administration.

13. Light tower, view north northeast, Whitehead Light Station, Spruce Head, 1991. Richard Cheek, photographer.

14. Light tower, view northeast, Libby Island Light Station, Machiasport, 1991. Richard Cheek, photographer.

15. Light tower, view southwest, Mount Desert Rock Light Station, Frenchboro, 1990. Richard Cheek, photographer.

16. Keeper's house, shed, covered passageway, and light tower, Monhegan Island Light Station, Monhegan, 1990. Richard Cheek, photographer.

17. Keeper's house, oil house, shed, storage building, and light tower, Petit Manan Light Station, Milbridge, 1990. Richard Cheek, photographer.

18. Matinicus Lighthouse #5, 1856 by W. B. Franklin. Records of the U. S. Coast Guard, Record Group 26, Lighthouse Plans; Maine. National Archives and Records Administration.

19. Light tower/keeper's house and abandoned light tower, view northwest, Matinicus Rock Light Station, Matinicus, 1992. Richard Cheek, photographer. Library of Congress, Prints and Photographs Division, HABS ME,7–MATI.V,1–1.

20. Seguin Island Lighthouse #1, 1856, by W. B. Franklin. Records of the U. S. Coast Guard, Record Group 26, Lighthouse Plans; Maine. National Archives and Records Administration.

21. Keeper's house and light tower, view south, Seguin Light Station, Popham Beach, 1991. Richard Cheek, photographer. Library of Congress, Prints and Photographs Division, HABS ME,12–POBE,V,1–4.

22. Portrait of W. B. Franklin, 1860s. R. S. DeLamater, photographer. Maine Historic Preservation Commission.

23. Keeper's house and light tower, Pumpkin Island Light Station, Eggemoggin vicinity, 1990. Richard Cheek, photographer.

24. Light tower and keeper's house, view west southwest, Tenants Harbor Light Station, Tenants Harbor vicinity, 1991. Richard Cheek, photographer. Library of Congress, Prints and Photographs Division, HABS ME,7–TEHA.V,1–3.

25. Light tower, view north, West Quoddy Head Light Station, Lubec vicinity, 1992. Richard Cheek, photographer.

26. Walkway and light tower, Marshall Point Light Station, Port Clyde, 1990. Richard Cheek, photographer.

27. Keeper's house and light tower, view east, Prospect Harbor Light Station, Prospect Harbor, 1990. Richard Cheek, photographer. Library of Congress, Prints and Photographs Division, HABS ME,5–PROHA,1–3.

28. Cape Elizabeth Fog Bell #1, 1853, by W. B. Franklin. Records of the U. S. Coast Guard, Record Group 26, Lighthouse Plans; Maine. National Archives and Records Administration.

29. Oil house, Wood Island Light Station, Biddeford Pool, 1991. Richard Cheek, photographer.

30. Keeper's house, small boathouse, light tower, and fog signal house, Great Duck Island Light Station, Frenchboro, 1991. Richard Cheek, photographer.

31. Boat house, detail of boat winch, Doubling Point Light Station, Arrowsic, 1989. Richard Cheek, photographer. Library of Congress, Prints and Photographs Division, HABS ME,12–AROW,1–9.

32. Bell house, view northwest, Hendrick's Head Light Station, Southport, 1989. Richard Cheek, photographer. Library of Congress, Prints and Photographs Division, HABS ME,8–SOPOR,1–6.

33. Bell tower, Whitlock's Mill Light Station, Calais, 1991. Richard Cheek, photographer.

34. Keeper's house, light tower, and bell house, Burnt Coat Harbor Light Station, Swan's Island, 1990. Richard Cheek, photographer.

35. Light tower and keeper's house, Grindel Point Light Station, Islesboro, 1989. Richard Cheek, photographer.

36. Light tower and keeper's house, view north, Rockland Breakwater Light Station, Rockland, 1991. Richard Cheek, photographer. Library of Congress, Prints and Photographs Division, HABS ME,7–ROCLA,6–2.

37. Light tower and corner of keeper's house, Burnt Coat Harbor Light Station, Swan's Island, 1990. Richard Cheek, photographer.

38. Keeper's house, light tower, and garage, view north, Fort Point Light Station, Stockton Springs, 1990. Richard Cheek, photographer. Library of Congress, Prints and Photographs Division, HABS ME,14–STOCSPR,1–5.

39. Light tower, Cape Elizabeth Light Station, Cape Elizabeth, 1989. Richard Cheek, photographer.

40. Portland Breakwater Lighthouse, South Portland, 1991. Richard Cheek, photographer.

41. Light tower, view west, Doubling Point Light Station, Arrowsic, 1989. Richard Cheek, photographer. Library of Congress, Prints and Photographs Division, HABS ME,12–AROW,1–2.

42. Southern light tower and walkway, Kennebec River Light Station, Arrowsic, 1989. Richard Cheek, photographer.

43. Lighthouse and oil house, Squirrel Point Light Station, Arrowsic, 1989. Richard Cheek, photographer.

44. Light tower, Isle Au Haut Light Station, Isle Au Haut, 1991. Richard Cheek, photographer.

45. Light tower, second floor with stairs to lantern, West Quoddy Head Light Station, Lubec vicinity, 1992. Richard Cheek, photographer.

46. Light tower, stairs looking up from first floor, Wood Island Light Station, Biddeford Pool vicinity, 1991. Richard Cheek, photographer.

47. Light tower, stairs from entrance, West Quoddy Head Light Station, Lubec vicinity, 1992. Richard Cheek, photographer.

48. Light tower, interior from entrance, Dice's Head Light Station, Castine, 1990. Richard Cheek, photographer.

49. Light tower, first floor and stairs from entrance, Owl's Head Light Station, Owl's Head, 1989. Richard Cheek, photographer.

50. Light tower, stairs with first and second landings, looking north from first floor, Whitlock's Mill Light Station, Calais, 1991. Richard Cheek, photographer.

51. Light tower, first floor and stairs from entrance, Doubling Point Light Station, Arrowsic, 1989. Richard Cheek, photographer.

52. Light tower, stairs to second floor, Little River Light Station, Cutler vicinity, 1991. Richard Cheek, photographer.

53. Light tower, stairs from entrance, Narraguagus Light Station, Milbridge vicinity, 1990. Richard Cheek, photographer.

54. Light tower, detail of stairs leading from first landing to cupola, Baker Island Light Station, Baker Island, 1990. Richard Cheek, photographer.

PRINCIPAL RESOURCES

U. S. Bureau of Lighthouses. *Annual Reports*. Washington, D. C.: U. S. Department of Commerce; issued annually from the mid-nineteenth century.

U. S. Bureau of Lighthouses. *List of Beacons, Buoys, Stokes and Other Day-Marks in the First Light-House District*. Washington, D. C.: U. S. Government Printing Office, various years, from 1840.

Lighthouse plans. Copies of original architectural drawings on file at the Maine Historic Preservation Commission, Augusta. Original plans on file at the National Archives and Records Administration and the United States Coast Guard, Civil Engineering Unit, Providence, Rhode Island.

All Alone and Ever Ready
The Lives and Legends of the Keepers

ILLUSTRATION SOURCES

1. Cover for the *Saturday Evening Post*, June 26, 1954, by Stevan Dohanos. Illustration © SEPS licensed by Curtis Licensing, Indianapolis, Indiana. All rights reserved. *Lighthouse Digest* archives.

2. "Christmas-Eve in a Light-House," from *Harper's Weekly*, December 30, 1876. Promised gift to Historic New England.

3. Keeper Charles L. Knight with children and dog Shep. Photographer unknown. *Lighthouse Digest* archives.

4. Postcard of Goose Rocks Light, c. 1910. Hugh C. Leighton Company, publishers. Maine Historic Preservation Commission.

5. Lighthouse, view northwest, Squirrel Point Light, Arrowsic, 1989. Richard Cheek, photographer. Library of Congress, Prints and Photographs Division, HABS ME,12–AROW, 3–4.

6. Captain Charles Knight, Hendrick's Head Light. Photographer unknown. *Lighthouse Digest* archives.

7. Postcard of Hendrick's Head Light, c. 1910. Hugh C. Leighton Company, publishers. Maine Historic Preservation Commission.

8. Group at Libby Island Light, c. 1910. Photographer unknown. *Lighthouse Digest* archives.

9. Willie Corbett and family in front of the bell tower at Little River Light. Photographer unknown. *Lighthouse Digest* archives.

10. The York family, Mount Desert Rock Light. Photographer unknown. Courtesy of Shirley Robinson. *Lighthouse Digest* archives.

11. Jasper Cheney with his family in a boat at Libby Island. Photographer unknown. *Lighthouse Digest* archives.

12. The Kenney and Kilton families, Libby Island, c. 1910. Photographer unknown. *Lighthouse Digest* archives.

13. Seven-year-old Shelia Woodward, daughter of Owl's Head keeper George Woodward, brushing her teeth while her mother pumps the water, 1946. Photographer unknown. Courtesy of the United States Coast Guard. *Lighthouse Digest* archives.

14. Gleason Colbeth with grandson Julian, dog Flash, and an unidentified woman, Little River Light. Photographer unknown. *Lighthouse Digest* archives.

15. Shirley and Bill York, ages eight and six, beside the tower on Mount Desert Rock, 1930s. Photographer unknown. *Lighthouse Digest* archives.

16. Lewis F. Sawyer, keeper at Egg Rock Light (1889–1899) and Bear Island Light (1899–1909), with his family. Photographer unknown. *Lighthouse Digest* archives.

17. Augustus Kelley holding son Albert, Bessie Kelley, Gracie Fagonde, Pierre Fagonde, Alma Bunker, Irv Bunker, Petit Manan Light. Photographer unknown. *Lighthouse Digest* archives.

18. Detail from the cover of *The Youth's Companion Combined with American Boy*, December 1935. Edgar Franklin Wittmack, artist. Promised gift to Historic New England.

19. Edward Rowe Snow with his wife and daughter, 1967. Courtesy of Dorothy Snow Bicknell. Promised gift to Historic New England.

20. Robert Thayer Sterling with dog Chang at Portland Head Light. Photographer unknown. *Lighthouse Digest* archives.

21. Cover of *Lighthouse Dog to the Rescue* by Angeli Perrow, and Emily Harris, illustrator. (Camden, Maine: Down East Books, 2000.) Used by permission of Down East Books and available at www.downeastbooks.com. Private collection.

22. Photomechanical print of the dog Nemo in "The 'Fog-Bark' of Heron Neck," from *The Youth's Companion*, August 19, 1909. Promised gift to Historic New England.

23. Memorial stone for Spot, the hero lighthouse dog, 2005. Photographer unknown. *Lighthouse Digest* archives.

24. "The Breakwater," in "Heroism in the Lighthouse Service: A Description of Life on Matinicus Rock," from *Century Magazine*, June 1897. J. Tinkey, engraver. Promised gift to Historic New England.

25. Isaac Grant. Photographer unknown. *Lighthouse Digest* archives.

26. Abbie Burgess's gravesite, Spruce Head, 2010. Richard Cheek, photographer.

27. Abbie Burgess. Photographer unknown. *Lighthouse Digest* archives.

28. The *Annie C. Maguire* aground at Portland Head Light, 1886. Philip Henry Brown, photographer. Maine Historic Preservation Commission.

29. Joshua Strout, keeper at Portland Head Light (1869–1904). Photographer unknown. *Lighthouse Digest* archives.

30. A tablet in memory of the *Annie C. Maguire* made by John A. Strout when he was assistant keeper at Portland Head Light, January 1912. Photographer unknown. *Lighthouse Digest* archives.

31. Roscoe Johnson, keeper of Little River Light (1856–1898) and Libby Island Light (1898–1901). Photographer unknown. *Lighthouse Digest* archives.

32. Frank Lewis Cotton, Spring Point Ledge Light, 1902. Photographer unknown. *Lighthouse Digest* archives.

33. William H. Woodward, a keeper who served at the Isles of Shoals, Manana Island, Seguin, Monhegan Island, and Doubling Point. Photographer unknown. *Lighthouse Digest* archives.

34. Gleason Colbeth and John Olson. Photographer unknown. *Lighthouse Digest* archives.

35. Jarvel B. Pinkham (1881–1943), Egg Rock Light. Photographer unknown. Courtesy of Mary P. Smith. *Lighthouse Digest* archives.

36. Joseph Strout. Photographer unknown. *Lighthouse Digest* archives.

37. Robert Thayer Sterling and Frank Hilt. Photographer unknown. *Lighthouse Digest* archives.

38. Keeper's house, light tower, and shed, Petit Manan Light, Milbridge, 1990. Richard Cheek, photographer.

39. Captain Herman M. Ingalls (1875–1965), Superintendent of the Second Lighthouse District. Photographer unknown. Courtesy of Lois Sprague. *Lighthouse Digest* archives.

40. Eugene Ingalls, his wife, Inez, with daughter Rita on her lap, and daughter Allison. Photographer unknown. *Lighthouse Digest* archives.

41. Wesley Dalzell getting ready to leave Egg Rock for the last time shortly after his father Clinton, assistant keeper, drowned, 1935. Photographer unknown. *Lighthouse Digest* archives.

42. Postcard of Egg Rock Light, c. 1910. Hugh C. Leighton Company, publisher. Maine Historic Preservation Commission.

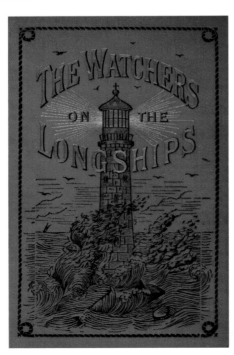

43. Clinton Dalzell in uniform of U. S. Lighthouse Service at Egg Rock, shortly before his death, 1934. Photographer unknown. *Lighthouse Digest* archives.

44. "Passage of the Lifecar," from *Frank Leslie's Popular Monthly*, February 1878. Promised gift to Historic New England.

45. Loring Myers, Lubec Channel Light keeper. Photographer unknown. Courtesy of Dorothy Pickard. *Lighthouse Digest* archives.

46. The Myers Lifeboat. Photographer unknown. *Lighthouse Digest* archives.

47. Eider duck decoy carved by Gus Wilson. David Allen, photographer. Image courtesy of Copley Fine Art Auctions, LLC. Private collection.

48. Portrait of Gus Wilson. Photographer unknown. Courtesy of Jeremy D'Entremont.

49. Tiger carving by Gus Wilson. Dave Hoffman, photographer. Image courtesy of Copley Fine Art Auctions, LLC. Private collection.

50. Preening raised-wing black duck decoy carved by Gus Wilson. David Allen, photographer. Image courtesy of Copley Fine Art Auctions, LLC. Private collection.

51. Keeper Elson Small milking the cow at St. Croix River Light. Photographer unknown. *Lighthouse Digest* archives.

52. Furniture moving on Great Duck Island, 1920s. Photographer unknown. Courtesy of Alberta Willey. *Lighthouse Digest* archives.

53. Keeper Joseph Strout beside his flower garden at Portland Head Light. Photographer unknown. *Lighthouse Digest* archives.

54. "The Lighthouse Keeper," from *Life*, May 21, 1925. Charles Dana Gibson, illustrator. *Lighthouse Digest* archives.

55. Elson Small driving a "taxi," St. Croix River Light. Photographer unknown. Courtesy of Connie Small. *Lighthouse Digest* archives.

56. "A Jig in the Keeper's Parlor," in "Heroism in the Lighthouse Service: A Description of Life on Matinicus Rock," from *Century Magazine*, June 1897. Peter Aitken, engraver. Promised gift to Historic New England.

57. Women hanging clothes, Great Duck Island. Photographer unknown. *Lighthouse Digest* archives.

58. The keeper gets a haircut from his wife at Owl's Head Light. Photographer unknown. *Lighthouse Digest* archives.

59. Assistant keeper with a hay cart at Great Duck Island. Courtesy of Alberta Willey. Photographer unknown. *Lighthouse Digest* archives.

60. Postcard of Seguin Island Light, c. 1910. Hugh C. Leighton Company, publishers. Maine Historic Preservation Commission.

61. Sheet music cover for "By the Sea," 1945. Music by Berenice Benson Bentley. Summy-Birchard Company, publishers. *Lighthouse Digest* archives.

62. *The Lighthouse-Keeper's Daughter* by Norman Rockwell, cover of *The Literary Digest*, July 28, 1923. Reproduced by courtesy of the Norman Rockwell Family Agency, Inc. *Lighthouse Digest* archives.

63. Robert Thayer Sterling at Portland Head Light. Photographer unknown. Courtesy of John Sterling. *Lighthouse Digest* archives.

ENDNOTE

1. Excerpts from "It's Brasswork, the Light-Keeper's Lament," by Frederic Morong, Jr., 1935. From *Ghost Lights of Lake Erie* by Timothy Harrison (East Machias, Maine: FogHorn Publishing, 2010), 169.

> Oh what is the bane of a lightkeeper's life
> That causes him worry, struggle and strife,
> That makes him use cuss words and nag on his wife?
> It's BRASSWORK
> · · · · · · · ·
> The devil himself could never invent,
> A material causing more world wide lament,
> And in Uncle Sam's service about ninety percent
> Is BRASSWORK
> · · · · · · · ·

> The machinery, clockwork, and fog signal bell,
> The coal hods, the dustpans, the pump in the well,
> No I'll leave it to you mates . . . If this isn't . . . well,
> BRASSWORK

> I dig, scrub and polish, and work with a might,
> And just when I get it all shining and bright,
> In come the fog like a thief in the night,
> Goodbye BRASSWORK
> · · · · · · · ·

> Oh, why should the spirit of mortal be proud,
> In the short span of life that he is allowed,
> If all the lining in every dark cloud,
> Is BRASSWORK

> And when I have polished until I am cold,
> And I have taken my oath to the Heavenly fold,
> Will my harp and my crown be made of pure gold?
> No! BRASSWORK

PRINCIPAL RESOURCES

Personal collection of Timothy Harrison and archives of *Lighthouse Digest*, the lighthouse history and news magazine.

Children, Lighthouses, and Lifeboats
Stories of Danger and Rescue at Sea

ILLUSTRATION SOURCES

1. Cover of *The Boy with the U. S. Life Savers* by Francis Rolt-Wheeler. (Boston: Lothrop, Lee and Shepard Company, 1915.) Author's collection.

2. Cover of *The Young Sailor; or the Sea-Life of Tom Bowline*. (New York: J. S. Redfield, c. 1835.) Author's collection.

3. Cover of *The Sailor Boy; or, the First and Last Voyage of Little Andrew*. (Portland [Maine]: Bailey and Noyes, c. 1840.) Author's collection.

4. Cover of *The Young Sailor Boy*. (London: Dean and Son, c. 1850.) Author's collection.

5. Engraving of the Eddystone Light from *The New Picture Primer; or, Child's First Reading Book* by Theodore Dwight, Jr. (New London, Conn.: Bolles and Williams, c. 1844.) Historic New England Library and Archives.

6. Engraving of the Eddystone Light from *The Book of Curiosities* by Alice Hawthorne. (Philadelphia: Charles H. Davis, 1855.) Author's collection.

7. Engraving from *The Sailor Boy* by Miss Corner. (London: Dean and Son, c. 1855.) Author's collection.

8. Chromolithograph from *The Young Sailor Boy*. (London: Dean and Son, c. 1850.) Author's collection.

9. Engraving from *Home Pictures*. (New York: American Tract Society, c. 1875.) Author's collection.

10. Cover of *Perils of the Ocean, or Disasters of the Seas*. (New York: Murphy, c. 1835.) Author's collection.

11. Frontispiece and title page from *Shipwrecks and Disasters at Sea, or Historical Narratives of the Most Noted Calamities, and Providential Deliverances from Fire and Famine* compiled by Charles Ellms. (Philadelphia: Jesper Harding, 1846.) Author's collection.

12. Illustration from the title page of *Cast Away in the Cold: An Old Man's Story of a Young Man's Adventures* by Dr. Isaac I. Hayes. (Boston: Lee and Shepard, 1888.) Author's collection.

13. "The Grosvenor, on the Coast of Caffraran," from *Shipwrecks and Disasters at Sea, or Historical Narratives of the Most Noted Calamities, and Providential Deliverances from Fire and Famine* compiled by Charles Ellms. (Philadelphia: Jesper Harding, 1846.) Author's collection.

Films, by Wheaties, "The Breakfast of Champions." Promised gift to Historic New England.

64. Cover of *All Among the Light-Houses* by Mary Bradford Crowninshield. (Boston: D. Lothrop and Company, 1886.) *Lighthouse Digest* archives.

65. Cover of *Keepers of the Sea* by Lewis E. Theiss. (Boston: W. A. Wilde, 1927.) Author's collection.

66. Cover of *Sentinels of the Sea* by Francis C. Owen. (Dansville, New York.: F. A. Owen Publishing Company, 1926.) Author's collection.

67. Cover of *Sentries of the Sea* by John J. Floherty. (Philadelphia: J. B. Lippincott Company, 1942.) Author's collection.

68. Cover of *The Story of Lighthouses* by Mary Ellen Chase. Erwin Schachner, engraver. (New York : Norton, 1965.) Author's collection.

69. Cover of *Treasure Chest of Fun and Fact*, Volume 21, Number 9. December 30, 1965. *Lighthouse Digest* archives.

70. Title page of "The Lighthouse: Sentinel of Strength and Trust," by Helen Gillum from *Treasure Chest of Fun and Fact*, Volume 21, Number 9. December 30, 1965. *Lighthouse Digest* archives.

71. Frontispiece and title page from *The Young Sailor; or, Perseverance Rewarded; for Little Boys and Girls* by Mrs. Hughs. (Philadelphia: Lindsay and Blakiston, 1850.) Author's collection.

72. Illustration from *Abbie Against the Storm* by Marcia Vaughan, illustrated by Bill Farnsworth. (Portland, Oreg.: Beyond Words Publishers, 1999.) Reprinted with the permission of Aladdin/Beyond Words, an imprint of Simon and Schuster Children's Publishing Division. Illustrations © 1999 Bill Farnsworth. Author's collection.

73. Cover of *The Lighthouse Keeper's Daughter* by Arielle North Olson, illustrated by Elaine Wentworth. (Mystic, Conn.: Mystic Seaport, 2004.) Author's collection.

74. Cover of *Abbie Against the Storm* by Marcia Vaughan, illustrated by Bill Farnsworth. (Portland, Oreg.: Beyond Words Publishers, 1999.) Reprinted with the permission of Aladdin/Beyond Words, an imprint of Simon and Schuster Children's Publishing Division. Illustrations © 1999 Bill Farnsworth. Author's collection.

75. Cover of *The Stormy Adventures of Abbie Burgess, Lighthouse Keeper* by Connie and Peter Roop, adapted by Amanda Doering Tourville, illustrated by Zachary Trover. Text and illustrations © 2011 by Lerner Publishing Group, Inc. Reprinted with the permission of Graphic Universe, a division of Lerner Publishing Group, Inc. All rights reserved. No part of this excerpt may be used or reproduced in any manner whatsoever without the prior written permission of Lerner Publishing Group, Inc. Author's collection.

ADDITIONAL RESOURCES

Ballantyne, R. M. *Battles with the Sea; or, Heroes of the Lifeboat and Rocket*. London: James Nisbet and Company, 1883.

Ballantyne, R. M. *The Floating Light of the Goodwin Sands*. Philadelphia: Claxton, Remsen and Haffelfinger, 1871.

Ballantyne, R. M. *Saved by the Lifeboat: A Tale of Wreck and Rescue on the Coast*. London: James Nisbet and Company, Limited, n.d.

Ballantyne, R. M. *The Story of the Rock: Building on the Eddystone*. London: James Nisbet and Company, Limited, n.d.

Bridges, T. C. *The Young Folk's Book of the Sea*. Boston: Little, Brown, and Company, 1928.

Daunt, Achilles. *Our Sea-Coast Heroes; or, Tales of Wreck and Rescue by the Lifeboat and Rocket*. London: T. Nelson and Sons, 1889.

DeWire, Elinor, editor. "Annotated and Illustrated Bibliography of Children's Lighthouse Books," undated typescript available on the Internet.

Drysdale, William. *The Beach Patrol: A Story of the Life-Saving Service*. Boston and Chicago: W. A. Wilde Company, 1897.

Falconer, William. *The Shipwreck*. London: T. Nelson and Sons, 1887.

Fraser, Chelsea. *The Story of Engineering in America*. New York: Thomas Y. Crowell Company, 1928.

Golding, Harry, ed. *The Wonder Book of Engineering Wonders*. London and Melbourne: Ward, Lock and Company, c. 1928.

Green, Martin. *Dreams of Adventure, Deeds of Empire: A Wide-Ranging and Provocative Examination of the Great Tradition of the Literature of Adventure*. London and Henley: Routledge and Kegan Paul, 1980.

Hervey, Eleanora Louisa. *The Rock Light; or, Duty Our Watchword*. London: Frederick Warne and Company, c. 1870.

Ilsley, Charles P., "The Lightkeeper," in *Forest and Shore; or, Legends of the Pine-Tree State*. Boston: John P. Jewett and Company, 1856.

Langille, J. H. *The Light-house Boy*. New York: American Tract Society, 1864.

Layson, J. F. *Memorable Shipwrecks and Seafaring Adventures of the Nineteenth Century*. Preston: Walter Leigh, 1884.

The Lighthouse. Boston: Lee and Shepard, 1863.

"The Lighthouse," in *The Blossom: A Christmas and New Year's Gift*. New York: Leavitt and Allen, 1855.

Otis, James. *The Light Keepers: A Story of the United States Light-House Service*. New York: E. P. Dutton and Company, 1906.

Quayle, Eric. *The Collector's Book of Boys' Stories*. London: Studio Vista, 1973.

Rand, Edward A. *A Candle in the Sea; or, Winter at Seal's Head*. New York: Thomas Whittaker, 1892.

Rand, Edward A. *Fighting the Sea; or Winter at the Life-Saving Station*. New York: Thomas Whittaker, 1887.

Sangster, Margaret E. "The Light-house Lamp," in *Holiday Stories for Young People*. Compiled and edited by Margaret E. Sangster. New York: The Christian Herald, 1896.

The Boy's Book of Shipwrecks and Ocean Stories, Illustrating the Dangers and Hardships Incidental to a Nautical Life. Philadelphia: J. B. Smith and Company, 1860 (first edition, 1851).

Thomas, R. *Interesting and Authentic Narratives of the Most Memorable Shipwrecks, Fires, Famines, Calamities, Providential Deliverances, and Lamentable Disasters on the Seas in Most Parts of the World*. Hartford, Conn.: Silas Andrus and Son, 1835.

Thrilling Narratives of Mutiny, Murder and Piracy. New York: Hurst and Company, 1830s.

Timbs, John. *Wonderful Inventions: From the Mariner's Compass to the Electric Telegraph Cable*. London: George Routledge and Sons, 1868.

Walton, Mrs. F. O. *Saved at Sea: A Lighthouse Story*. New York: American Tract Society, 1877.

Wyckoff, Capwell. *The Mercer Boys on the Beach Patrol*. Cleveland, Ohio: The World Publishing Company, 1929.

The author gives special thanks to Laura Wasowitz, Curator of Children's Literature at the American Antiquarian Society, Worcester, Massachusetts, for her wonderful advice and assistance.

Nation, Home, and Heaven
The Moral Significance of Lighthouses

ILLUSTRATION SOURCES

1. Poster, "Liberty / Democracy: Don't Let that Light Go Out," 1940. Think American Institute, poster number 60. Kelly-Read and Company, publisher. Author's collection.

2. Sign for The Grace Church, Rockland, 2010. Richard Cheek, photographer.

3. Trade card for Eureka Granulated Soap, "The Seven Wonders of the World: The Mausoleum," late nineteenth century. Promised gift to Historic New England.

4. Trade card for Eureka Granulated Soap, "The Seven Wonders of the World: The Pharos Watch Tower," late nineteenth century. Promised gift to Historic New England.

5. Trade card for Eureka Granulated Soap, "The Seven Wonders of the World: The Statue of Jupiter Olympus," late nineteenth century. Promised gift to Historic New England.

6. "The Lands Around the Mediterranean Sea Showing the Principal Lighthouses of the Ancient World" from *Lighthouses* by Arthur Smith with illustrations by the author. (Boston: Houghton Mifflin, 1971.) © 1971 by Arthur Smith. Reprinted by permission of Houghton Mifflin Harcourt Publishing Company. All rights reserved. Author's collection.

7. "The Morning after A Storm at S. W.," title page engraving from *A Narrative of the Building and a Description of the Construction of the Edystone Lighthouse with Stone* by John Smeaton. (London: G. Nicol, 1793.) Promised gift to Historic New England.

8. Cover of *The American Legion Monthly*, January 1937. *Lighthouse Digest* archives.

9. Cover of *Beacon Lights of Patriotism* by Henry B. Carrington. (New York: Silver, Burdett and Company, 1894.) Promised gift to Historic New England.

10. Cover of *America the Beautiful* by Katherine Lee Bates, illustrated by Chris Gall. (Boston: Little, Brown, 2004.) Used by permission. Author's collection.

11. Patriotic envelope printed with "Victory Ahead! Seek Out the Enemy and Destroy Him!" 1945. Author's collection.

12. Envelope with First Day of Issue stamp: " . . . from sea to shining sea," 1981. *Lighthouse Digest* archives.

13. Frontispiece from *Le Littoral de la France: Côtes Vendéennes, De Lorient à La Rochelle* by V. Vattier D'Ambroyse. (Paris: Sanard et Derangeon, 1892.) Promised gift to Historic New England.

14. Trade card for Véritable Extrait de Viande Liebig, "Phares: Phare de Rotesand," late nineteenth century. Promised gift to Historic New England.

15. Trade card for Véritable Extrait de Viande Liebig, "Phares: Cap St. Vincent," late nineteenth century. Promised gift to Historic New England.

16. Trade card for Véritable Extrait de Viande Liebig, "Phares: Constantza," late nineteenth century. Promised gift to Historic New England.

17. Trade card for Véritable Extrait de Viande Liebig, "Phares: Phare de Messine," late nineteenth century. Promised gift to Historic New England.

18. Statue of Hope, Wilde Monument, 1852. Evergreen Cemetery, Portland, 2011. Richard Cheek, photographer.

19. "Hope" from *The Nobility of Life: Its Graces and Virtues*, edited by L. Valentine. Edward and George Dalziel, engravers. (London: Frederick Warne and Company; New York: Scribner, Welford, and Company, 1869.) Promised gift to Historic New England.

20. Statue of Hope, Abbot Monument, 1870. Mount Auburn Cemetery, Cambridge, Massachusetts, 2011. Richard Cheek, photographer.

21. "Hope. 'A Sail! A Sail!'" from *The Nobility of Life: Its Graces and Virtues*, edited by L. Valentine. Edward and George Dalziel, engravers. (London: Frederick Warne and Company; New York : Scrib-ner, Welford, and Company, 1869.) Promised gift to Historic New England.

22. A missionary card printed with a "Sailor's Hymn," late nineteenth century. Promised gift to Historic New England.

23. Title page of "An Address to Seamen, Delivered Before the Portland Marine Bible Society" by Reverend Edward Payson, D. D. from *The Publications of the American Tract Society*, Volume 5. (New York: American Tract Society, c. 1833.) Promised gift to Historic New England.

24. Receipt for a donation to the Western Seamen's Friend Society to help purchase bibles for sailors, 1860s. Promised gift to Historic New England.

25. Engraving of the Mariner's Church in Portland, from *The Monthly Repository and Library of Entertaining Knowledge*, Volume II. (New York: Francis S. Wiggins, 1832.) Maine Historic Preservation Commission.

26. Pages from *Signals for the Voyage of Life* by Fleming H. Revell. Poole and Coughman, lithographers, c. 1890. Promised gift to Historic New England.

27. "When the Foundation Goes, the Light is Doomed," cartoon from the *Christian Herald*, March 1938. R. O. Berg, illustrator. *Lighthouse Digest* archives.

28. Blessing poster stamp, "The Eternal God is thy refuge . . ." Art Card Company, Alameda, California, no. 37, early twentieth century. *Lighthouse Digest* archives.

29. "The human life voyage . . ." from *Beacon Lights for God's Mariners* by Elizabeth N. Little. (Boston: S. E. Cassino and Company, 1885.) Promised gift to Historic New England.

30. "I will make darkness light before them," from *Beacon Lights for God's Mariners* by Elizabeth N. Little. (Boston: S. E. Cassino and Company, 1885.) Promised gift to Historic New England.

31. "Death on Economy," cartoon from *Harper's Weekly*, December 29, 1877. Thomas Nast, illustrator. Promised gift to Historic New England.

32. "The United States Life Saving Service," from *Scientific American Supplement*, February 6, 1892. Promised gift to Historic New England.

33. Cover of *Heroes of the Storm* by William D. O'Connor. (Boston: Houghton, Mifflin and Company, 1904.) Author's collection.

34. Cover of *Storm Fighters* by J. D. Whiting. (Indianapolis: Bobbs-Merrill Company, 1927.) Author's collection.

35. "Perils of the Coast–The Life-Saving Service," from *Harper's Weekly*, April 16, 1881. M. J. Burns, illustrator. Historic New England Library and Archives.

36. "The Light that Fails," cartoon from *The Literary Digest*, November 14, 1925. Nelson Harding, illustrator. *Lighthouse Digest* archives.

37. Trade card for Beacon Light Oil, Beacon Oil Company, late nineteenth century. *Lighthouse Digest* archives.

38. Illustration from *Home Again*, edited by Lula Mae Walker. (Augusta, Maine: E. C. Allen and Company, 1891.) Author's collection.

39. Cover of *Home Again*, edited by Lula Mae Walker. (Augusta, Maine: E. C. Allen and Company, 1891.) Author's collection.

40. Certificate for the Portland Marine Society, issued to Captain Joseph Leavitt, 1840. Collection of Earle G. Shettleworth, Jr.

41. "Sending a Line Over a Wreck," from *Sea Pictures Drawn with Pen and Pencil* by James Macaulay. (London: Religious Tract Society, c. 1880.) Author's collection.

42. Trade card for Belding Brothers and Company's Life Saving Service, late nineteenth century. Promised gift to Historic New England.

43. Galilee Temple, Rockland, Reverend E. S. Ufford, Pastor, early twentieth century. Photographer unknown. Maine Historic Preservation Commission.

44. Patch for the U. S. Coast Guard Station, Boothbay Harbor. Maine Lighthouse Museum, Rockland.

45. Patch for the Cape Elizabeth Fire-Police. Maine Lighthouse Museum, Rockland.

46. Patch for the U. S. Coast Guard Station, South Portland. Maine Lighthouse Museum, Rockland.

47. Patch for Lubec, "Most Easterly Point." Maine Lighthouse Museum, Rockland.

48. Patch for the Rockland Police. Maine Lighthouse Museum, Rockland.

49. Patch for the Lincoln County Sheriff. *Lighthouse Digest* archives.

50. Patch for the Maine U. S. Marshal. *Lighthouse Digest* archives.

51. Patch for the U. S. Coast Guard, Rockland Station. Maine Lighthouse Museum, Rockland.

52. Patch for the U. S. Coast Guard ANT [Aids to Navigation Team], South Portland. Maine Lighthouse Museum, Rockland.

53. U. S. Coast Guard poster, "Noël ~ All's Well," 1940. Author's collection.

ADDITIONAL RESOURCES

Adams, W. H. Davenport. *Lighthouses and Lightships: Descriptive and Historical Account of their Mode of Construction and Organization.* London: T. Nelson and Sons, 1870.

Beacon Lights Along the Shores of Life. London: G. Morrish, n.d.

Hardy, W. J. *Lighthouses: Their History and Romance.* London: The Religious Tract Society, 1895.

Heap, D. P. *Ancient and Modern Light-Houses.* Boston: Ticknor and Company, 1889.

Putnam, George R. *Lighthouses and Lightships of the United States.* Boston and New York: Houghton Mifflin Company, 1917.

Renard, Léon. *Les Phares.* Paris: Librairie Hachette et Cie., 1881.

The author wishes to express gratitude to William David Barry, Reference Assistant in the Library of the Maine Historical Society, for providing information and thoughtful advice for this article.

"Steadfast, Serene, Immovable"
The Maine Lighthouse in American Art

ILLUSTRATION SOURCES

1. Charles Codman (American, 1800–1842). *Seascape with Lighthouse* (detail). 1837. Oil on canvas. 18 × 24⅛ in. Delaware Art Museum, Bequest of Elizabeth Wales, 1951.

2. Edward Hopper painting Lighthouse Hill, at Two Lights near Cape Elizabeth, Maine, 1927. Gelatin silver print. © The Arthayer R. Sanborn Hopper Collection Trust—2005. Whitney Museum of American Art, New York.

3. Charles Codman (American, 1800–1842). *Seascape with Lighthouse*. 1837. Oil on canvas. 18 × 24⅛ in. Delaware Art Museum, Bequest of Elizabeth Wales, 1951.

4. Thomas Doughty (American, 1793–1856). *Desert Rock Lighthouse.* 1847. Oil on canvas. 27 × 41 in. Collection of the Newark Museum. Gift of Mrs. Jennie E. Mead, 1939. 39.146.

5. Nathaniel Currier and James Merritt Ives (American, 1857–1907). *American Coast Scene, Desert Rock Lighthouse.* Nineteenth century. © Shelburne Museum, Shelburne, Vermont.

6. Postcard of Mount Desert Rock Light, Maine, 1907. Hugh C. Leighton Company, publishers. Maine Historic Preservation Commission.

7. Fitz Henry Lane (American, 1804–1865). *Owl's Head, Penobscot Bay, Maine.* 1862. Oil on canvas. 15¾ × 26⅛ in. Museum of Fine Arts, Boston. Bequest of Martha C. Karolik for the M. and M. Karolik Collection of American Paintings, 1815–1865, 48.448. Photograph © 2012 Museum of Fine Arts, Boston.

8. Postcard of Winslow Homer Studio, Prout's Neck, Maine, c. 1911. V. T. Shaw, publisher. Courtesy of Maine Historic Preservation Commission.

9. Winslow Homer (American, 1836–1910). *Wild Geese in Flight.* 1897. Oil on canvas, 33⅞ × 49¾ in. Portland Museum of Art, Maine. Bequest of Charles Shipman Payson, 1988.55.2.

10. Winslow Homer (American, 1836–1910) *Moonlight, Wood Island Light.* 1894. Oil on canvas, 30¾ × 40¼ in. Gift of George A. Hearn, in memory of Arthur Hoppock Hearn, 1911 (11.116.2). The Metropolitan Museum of Art, New York. Image © The Metropolitan Museum of Art / Art Resource, New York.

11. Edward Hopper (American, 1882–1967). *Captain Strout's House, Portland Head.* 1927. Opaque and transparent watercolor over graphite on wove paper. 14 × 20 in. The Ella Gallup Sumner and Mary Catlin Sumner Collection Fund. 1928.3. Wadsworth Atheneum Museum of Art, Hartford, Connecticut. Image © Wadsworth Atheneum Museum of Art / Art Resource, New York.

12. Edward Hopper (American, 1882–1967). *The Lighthouse at Two Lights.* 1929. Oil on canvas, 29½ × 43¼ in. Hugo Kastor Fund, 1962 (62.95). The Metropolitan Museum of Art, New York. Image © The Metropolitan Museum of Art / Art Resource, New York.

13. Maine Statehood First Day of Issue Stamp, 1970. *Lighthouse Digest* archives.

14. Yasuo Kuniyoshi (American, born Japan, 1889–1953). *The Swimmer.* c. 1924. Oil on canvas. 20½ × 30½ in. Columbus Museum of Art, Ohio: Gift of Ferdinand Howald. 1931.196. Art © Estate of Yasuo Kuniyoshi / Licensed by VAGA, New York.

15. Warren Gould Roby (attributed). Weathervane. 1850–1875. Wayland, Massachusetts. © Shelburne Museum, Shelburne, Vermont.

16. Marsden Hartley (American, 1877–1943). *The Lighthouse.* 1940–41. Oil on composition board. 30 × 40⅛ in. Collection of J. R. and Barbara Hyde.

17. Andrew Wyeth (American, 1917–2009). *Sailor's Valentine.* 1985. Watercolor. 21½ × 29⅝ in. Private Collection. ©Andrew Wyeth.

18. Jamie Wyeth (American, b. 1946). *Comet.* 1997. Oil on panel. 48 × 40 in. © Jamie Wyeth.

19. Jamie Wyeth (American, b. 1946). *The Lighthouse.* 1993. Oil on panel. 30 × 40 in. © Jamie Wyeth.

20. Cover of *Down East*, July 1959. Stell and Shevis, illustrators. Courtesy of Down East Enterprise, Inc., Camden, Maine. Promised gift to Historic New England.

21. Cover of *Down East*, May 1960. Victor Mays, illustrator. Courtesy of Down East Enterprise, Inc., Camden, Maine. Promised gift to Historic New England.

22. Cover of *Down East*, August 1962. Henry R. Martin, illustrator. Courtesy of Down East Enterprise, Inc., Camden, Maine. Promised gift to Historic New England.

23. Cover of *Down East*, March 1963. Henry R. Martin, illustrator. Courtesy of Down East Enterprise, Inc., Camden, Maine. Promised gift to Historic New England.

24. Cover of *Down East*, May 1965. Richard Noble, illustrator. Courtesy of Down East Enterprise, Inc., Camden, Maine. Promised gift to Historic New England.

25. Cover of *Down East*, May 1972. Edith Berry, artist. Courtesy of Down East Enterprise, Inc., Camden, Maine. Promised gift to Historic New England.

26. Cover of *Down East*, November 1977. *Hendricks Head Lighthouse* by Stephen Etnier. Courtesy of Down East Enterprise, Inc., Camden, Maine. Promised gift to Historic New England.

27. Cover of *Down East*, September 1983. *Warning Bell, Pemaquid Point* by Howard Etter. Courtesy of Down East Enterprise, Inc., Camden, Maine. Promised gift to Historic New England.

28. Cover of *Down East*, January 1964. Carroll Thayer Berry, illustrator. Courtesy of Down East Enterprise, Inc., Camden, Maine. Promised gift to Historic New England.

29. Cover for the *Saturday Evening Post*, August 26, 1950, by Stevan Dohanos. Illustration © SEPS licensed by Curtis Licensing, Indianapolis, Indiana. All rights reserved.

ENDNOTES

The quotation in the title of this chapter is taken from "The Lighthouse" by Henry Wadsworth Longfellow.

1. David C. Miller, *American Iconology* (New Haven: Yale University Press, 1993), 188.

2. Earle G. Shettleworth, Jr., Jessica F. Nicoll, and Jessica Skwire Routhier, *Charles Codman: The Landscape of Art and Culture in 19th-Century Maine* (Portland, Maine: Portland Museum of Art, 2002), 20–21.

3. John Wilmerding, *The Artist's Mount Desert: American Painters of the Maine Coast* (Princeton: Princeton University Press, 1994), 21.

4. Lucinda Gedeon, *Ships and Shoreline: William Bradford and Nineteenth-Century American Marine Painting* (Vero Beach: Vero Beach Museum of Art, 2010), 61.

5. John Wilmerding, *A History of American Marine Painting* (Boston: Little, Brown, and Company, 1968), 158.

PRINCIPAL RESOURCES

Kornhauser, Elizabeth M. *Marsden Hartley*. New Haven: Yale University Press, 2002.

Salatino, Kevin. *Edward Hopper's Maine*. Munich and New York: Prestel, 2011.

Shettleworth, Earle, Jr., Jessica F. Nicoll, and Jessica Skwire Routhier. *Charles Codman: The Landscape of Art and Culture in 19th-Century Maine*. Portland, Maine: Portland Museum of Art, 2002.

Truettner, William H., and Roger B. Stein. *Picturing Old New England: Image and Memory*. New Haven: Yale University Press, 1999.

Wilmerding, John. *The Artist's Mount Desert: American Painters of the Maine Coast*. Princeton: Princeton University Press, 1994.

The author would like to thank Earle G. Shettleworth, Jr., for once again opening his prodigious files and sharing his life-long research.

Frozen in Time
The Photography of Maine's Lighthouses

ILLUSTRATION SOURCES

1. John F. Singhi of Rockland with his camera, late nineteenth century. Photographer unknown. Maine Historic Preservation Commission.

2. Stereo view of group in front of Matinicus Rock Light, c. 1877. J. Henry Allen, photographer. Maine Historic Preservation Commission.

3. The Venerable Cunner Association and Propeller Club in front of Portland Head Light, August 3, 1858. Photographer unknown. Maine Historic Preservation Commission.

4. Ambrotype of a young mariner from Orland, c. 1860. Photographer unknown. Maine Historic Preservation Commission.

5. Pemaquid Point Light, 1859. William McLaughlin, photographer. Maine Historic Preservation Commission.

6. Deer Island Thoroughfare Light, 1859. William McLaughlin, photographer. National Archives and Records Administration.

7. Whitehead Light, 1859. William McLaughlin, photographer. National Archives and Records Administration.

8. Cape Elizabeth Light, 1859. William McLaughlin, photographer. Maine Historic Preservation Commission.

9. Hendrick's Head Light, 1859. William McLaughlin, photographer. National Archives and Records Administration.

10. Verso of F. H. Crockett's stereo view of Owl's Head Light, c. 1880. F. H. Crockett, publisher. Maine Historic Preservation Commission.

11. Stereo view of Owl's Head Light, c. 1880. F. H. Crockett, photographer. Maine Historic Preservation Commission.

12. Stereo view of Owl's Head Light, c. 1880. F. H. Crockett, photographer. Maine Historic Preservation Commission.

13. Stereo view of group in front of Matinicus Rock Light, 1877. J. Henry Allen, photographer. Maine Historic Preservation Commission.

14. Stereo view of Matinicus Rock Light, 1877. J. Henry Allen, photographer. Maine Historic Preservation Commission.

15. Stereo view of the northern tower, Matinicus Rock Light, 1877. J. Henry Allen, photographer. Maine Historic Preservation Commission.

16. Dice's Head Light, 1880s. A. H. Folsom, photographer. Maine Historic Preservation Commission.

17. Burnt Island Light and Pemaquid Point Light, from *New England's Seashore*, c. 1890. Boston and Maine Railroad, publisher. Maine Historic Preservation Commission.

18. Vignette from the cover of *The Coast of Maine*, 1889. Henry Peabody, photographer and publisher. Maine Historic Preservation Commission.

19. Petit Manan Light, c. 1890. Herbert Bamber, photographer. *Lighthouse Digest* archives.

20. Pond Island Light, mouth of the Kennebec River, c. 1889. Henry Peabody, photographer. Historic New England Library and Archives.

21. The steamer *Portland* at sea, 1891. Nathaniel L. Stebbins, photographer. Historic New England Library and Archives.

22. Cover of *The Illustrated Coast Pilot* by Nathaniel L. Stebbins, 1896. Historic New England Library and Archives.

23. Nathaniel L. Stebbins, c. 1917. Photographer unknown. Historic New England Library and Archives.

24. Page from *Lighthouses Along the Coast Between Portland and New York*, 1913. Maine Steamship Company, publisher. Maine Historic Preservation Commission.

25. Cover of *Lighthouses Along the Coast Between Portland and New York*, 1913. Maine Steamship Company, publisher. Maine Historic Preservation Commission.

26. Postcard of Half-way Rock Light, Casco Bay, c. 1910. Hugh C. Leighton Company, publisher. Maine Historic Preservation Commission.

27. Postcard of Cape Newagen, The Cuckolds, c. 1910. Hugh C. Leighton Company, publisher. Maine Historic Preservation Commission.

28. Verso of postcard of Cape Newagen, The Cuckolds, c. 1910. Hugh C. Leighton Company, publisher. Maine Historic Preservation Commission.

29. Postcard of Mount Desert, Bass Harbor Head Light, c. 1907. Hugh C. Leighton Company, publisher. Maine Historic Preservation Commission.

30. Monhegan Island Light, c. 1940. Lorimer E. Brackett, photographer. Maine Historic Preservation Commission.

31. Portland Head Light, c. 1940. Ralph F. Blood, photographer. Maine Historic Preservation Commission.

32. Moonrise at Portland Head Light, c. 1940. W. H. Ballard, photographer. Maine Historic Preservation Commission.

33. Monhegan Island Light, c. 1920. Joseph A. Labbie, photographer. Maine Historic Preservation Commission.

34. Monhegan Island Light, c. 1920. McDougall and Keefe, photographers. Maine Historic Preservation Commission.

35. Verso of photographic postcard published by Eastern Illustrating Company, Belfast, c. 1915. Maine Historic Preservation Commission.

36. Verso of photographic postcard published by Eastern Illustrating & Publishing Company, Belfast, c. 1915. Maine Historic Preservation Commission.

37. Postcard of Monhegan Island Light published by Eastern Illustrating Company, Belfast, c. 1915. Maine Historic Preservation Commission.

38. Lighthouse, view east-northeast, Spring Point Ledge Light, South Portland, 1989. Richard Cheek, photographer.

39. Lighthouse, view northeast, Spring Point Ledge Light, South Portland, 1989. Richard Cheek, photographer. Library of Congress, Prints and Photographs Division, HABS ME,3–PORTS,3–1.

40. Lighthouse, view from lower gallery, Spring Point Ledge Light, South Portland, 1989. Richard Cheek, photographer. Library of Congress, Prints and Photographs Division, HABS ME,3–PORTS,3–4.

41. Lighthouse, basement, Spring Point Ledge Light, South Portland, 1989. Richard Cheek, photographer. Library of Congress, Prints and Photographs Division, HABS ME,3–PORTS,3–5.

42. Lighthouse, detail of lens, Spring Point Ledge Light, South Portland, 1989. Richard Cheek, photographer. Library of Congress, Prints and Photographs Division, HABS ME,3–PORTS,3–8.

43. Lighthouse, doorway to second floor room, Spring Point Ledge Light, South Portland, 1989. Richard Cheek, photographer. Library of Congress, Prints and Photographs Division, HABS ME,3–PORTS,3–7.

44. Lighthouse, view east-northeast, Spring Point Ledge Light, South Portland, 1989. Richard Cheek, photographer. Library of Congress, Prints and Photographs Division, HABS ME,3–PORTS,3–3.

45. Light tower and keeper's house, Cape Neddick Light, Cape Neddick, 1989. Richard Cheek, photographer.

PRINCIPAL RESOURCES

Robinson, William F. *A Certain Slant of Light: The First Hundred Years of New England Photography*. Boston: New York Graphic Society, 1980.

Vaule, Rosamond B. *As We Were: American Photographic Postcards, 1905–1930*. Boston: David R. Godine, 2004.

Drawn to the Lights
How Lighthouses Became Maine's Greatest Tourist Attraction

ILLUSTRATION SOURCES

1. Cover of *Journeys Beautiful: The Magazine of Travel*, Maine Number, June 1925. Alfred Trueman, illustrator. Nomad Publishing Company, publisher. Promised gift to Historic New England.

2. Postcard of Cape Newagen, The Cuckolds, c. 1910. Maine Historic Preservation Commission.

3. Keepers, family members, and visitors at Boon Island during William C. Williams's tenure as principal keeper. Photographer unknown. Maine Maritime Museum, Bath.

4. Stereo view of group in front of Monhegan Island Light, c. 1880.

Henry Bailey, photographer. Maine Historic Preservation Commission.

5. Cover of *Beacon Lights: Guides to Wandering Steps*, 1886. Promised gift to Historic New England.

6. Cover of *Here and There in New England and Canada by the Boston and Maine Railroad* by M. F. Sweetser. (Boston: Passenger Department Boston and Maine Railroad, 1889). Maine Historic Preservation Commission.

7. Postcard of Cape Elizabeth, Portland Head Light and Cliffs, c. 1909. Hugh C. Leighton Company, publisher. Historic New England Library and Archives.

8. Cover of *Scenic Gems of Portland and Casco Bay*, c. 1908. G. W. Morris, publisher. Maine Historic Preservation Commission.

9. Chromolithograph of Portland Head Light from *Beacon Lights: Guides to Wandering Steps*, 1886. Harlow, artist. Obpacher, lithographer. Promised gift to Historic New England.

10. Old Orchard Beach and Portland, from *New England's Seashore*, c. 1890. Boston and Maine Railroad, publisher. Maine Historic Preservation Commission.

11. Cover of the brochure, "Maine: Land of Remembered Vacations," 1920s. State of Maine, publisher. Maine Historic Preservation Commission.

12. Cover of *Seeing the Eastern States* by John T. Faris. (Philadelphia: J. B. Lippincott Company, 1922.) Promised gift to Historic New England.

13. Cover of the brochure "Vacationland: An Illustrated Register of Hotels and Camps in Maine and New Hampshire," 1921. The Resort Proprietors and Passenger Traffic Department and Maine Central Railroad, publishers. Promised gift to Historic New England.

14. Cover of the "State of Maine" souvenir mailer, 1955. Historic New England Library and Archives.

15. Front and back covers of a brochure for Pilgrim Tours, All Expense, 1946. The New York, New Haven, and Hartford Railroad, publisher. Promised gift to Historic New England.

16. Advertisement for Greyhound Bus Tours, c. 1940. Promised gift to Historic New England.

17. Front and back covers of a brochure for Vacation Cruise Tours, 1941. Eastern Steamship Lines, publisher. Promised gift to Historic New England.

18. Advertisement for United Aircraft Corporation, c. 1957. Promised gift to Historic New England.

19. Detail of map in *Coastwise Cruising Guide*, c. 1938. Socony, Standard Oil Company of New York, publisher. Promised gift to Historic New England.

20. Cover of *Your Vacation in New England*, late 1930s. The New England Council, publisher. Promised gift to Historic New England.

21. Back cover of a map of Florida and Georgia, 1961. The Atlantic Refining Company, publisher. Promised gift to Historic New England.

22. Front cover of the map *New England with Special Maps of Cities*, 1960. Esso, publisher. *Lighthouse Digest* archives.

23. Detail of an advertisement for Lincoln automobiles, Ford Motor Company, 1950s. *Lighthouse Digest* archives.

24. Advertisement for the Franklin car, The Franklin Automobile Company, Syracuse, New York, 1919. *Lighthouse Digest* archives.

25. Advertisement for the Hudson automobile, Hudson Motor Car Company, Detroit, Michigan, 1946. *Lighthouse Digest* archives.

26. Advertisement for the Pontiac automobile, General Motors Corporation, 1953. Promised gift to Historic New England.

27. Advertisement for the Pontiac automobile, General Motors Corporation, 1955. Promised gift to Historic New England.

28. "The Famous Lighthouses of New England," late twentieth century. Larry O'Toole, illustrator. District Coast Guard Office, Boston, Massachusetts. Promised gift to Historic New England.

29. Cover of *Famous Lighthouses of New England* by Edward Rowe Snow. (Boston: The Yankee Publishing Company, 1945.) Promised gift to Historic New England.

30. Cover of *The Lighthouses of New England, 1716–1973* by Edward Rowe Snow. (New York: Dodd, Mead and Company, 1973.) Promised gift to Historic New England.
31. Collage of lighthouse-related books, guides, magazines, and promotional ephemera, arranged by Richard Cheek, 2011. Andrew Davis, photographer.

ADDITIONAL RESOURCES

Caldwell, Bill. *Lighthouses of Maine*. Portland, Maine: Gannett Books, 1986.

D'Entremont, Jeremy. *The Lighthouses of Maine*. Beverly, Mass.: Commonwealth Editions, 2009.

Snow, Edward Rowe. *Famous New England Lighthouses*. Boston, Mass.: Yankee Publishing, 1945.

Sterling, Robert Thayer. *Lighthouses of the Maine Coast and the Men Who Keep Them*. Brattleboro, Vt.: Stephen Daye Press, 1935.

Sweetser, M. F. *Picturesque Maine*. Portland, Maine: Chisholm Brothers, 1880.

Varney, Geo[rge] J. *A Gazetteer of the State of Maine*. Boston, Mass.: B. B. Russell, 1881.

Willoughby, Malcolm F. *Lighthouses of New England*. Boston, Mass.: T. O. Metcalf, 1929.

Beacons for Business
The Commercial Use of the Lighthouse Image

ILLUSTRATION SOURCES

1. Robert's Maine Grill, U. S. Route 1, Kittery, 2010. Richard Cheek, photographer.
2. Examples of lighthouse labeling for commercial products, twentieth century, 2010. Richard Cheek, photographer. Maine Lighthouse Museum, Rockland.
3. Advertisement for Lighthouse Cleanser, 1920s. Maine Lighthouse Museum, Rockland.
4. Product packaging for Lighthouse Cleanser, 1930s. Justin Goodstein-Aue, photographer. Promised gift to Historic New England.
5. Product packaging for Lighthouse White Naphtha Soap. Andrew Davis, photographer. Promised gift to Historic New England.
6. Trade card for Morse's Dyspepsia Cure, late nineteenth century. Promised gift to Historic New England.
7. Verso of advertisement for Smith, Stevenson and Company, Meriden, Connecticut, c. 1850. Promised gift to Historic New England.
8. Trade card for Smith, Stevenson and Company, Meriden, Connecticut, c. 1850. J. H. Bufford, lithographer. Promised gift to Historic New England.
9. Trade card for L. J. Wheelden, Bangor, c. 1850. J. H. Bufford, lithographer. Promised gift to Historic New England.
10. Trade card for Ruberoid Roofing, c. 1905. Promised gift to Historic New England.
11. Label for Lighthouse Brand, Pinellas County's Finest Oranges, Grapefruit, Tangerines, David Bilgore and Company, Clearwater, Florida, 1930s. Promised gift to Historic New England.
12. Trade card for Soapine, late nineteenth century. Donaldson Brothers, printers. Promised gift to Historic New England.
13. Advertisement for Pears Soap, 1908. *Lighthouse Digest* archives.
14. Trade card for Warner's Safe Yeast, late nineteenth century. Mensing and Stecher, lithographers. Promised gift to Historic New England.
15. Advertisement for Early, Cloud and Company, an IBM company, late twentieth century. *Lighthouse Digest* archives.
16. Postcard advertisement for Johnson Sea-Horse Outboard Motors, c. 1960. Maine Historic Preservation Commission.
17. Advertisement for Kellogg's Corn Flakes, 1962. Promised gift to Historic New England.

18. Advertisement for the Chevelle, 1972. *Lighthouse Digest* archives.
19. Advertisement featuring Movado watches, late twentieth century. *Lighthouse Digest* archives.
20. Cover of *An Elegy Written in a Country Churchyard* by Thomas Gray. (Providence: Shepard and Company, c. 1890.) Promised gift to Historic New England.
21. UNUM logo, 1980s. This abstracted version of the Union Mutual lighthouse logo was introduced in the early 1980s and remained in use after the company was taken public in 1986. UNUM Archives.
22. Section from a corporate poster produced by UNUM after it introduced a new Portland Head Light logo in the late 1990s. UNUM Archives.
23. Union Mutual letterhead for its February-March 1899 newsletter. Maine Historic Preservation Commission.
24. Salesman's giveaway matchbook provided to insurance agencies by Union Mutual, c. 1950. *Lighthouse Digest* archives.
25. Two-page center spread from booklet "Taking Your Bearings," Metropolitan Life Insurance Company, 1920s. Promised gift to Historic New England.
26. Haven's Candies entry, Hannaford Brothers Company Parade of Lighthouses art project, 2003. Dave G. Hall, artist. State Route 22, Westbrook, 2010. Richard Cheek, photographer.
27. Dolphin Mini Golf lighthouse, State Route 27, south of Boothbay, 2010. Richard Cheek, photographer.
28. Lighthouse mural, Christmas Tree Shops, Scarborough, 2010. Richard Cheek, photographer.
29. Oakhurst Dairy entry, Hannaford Brothers Company Parade of Lighthouses art project, 2003. Roger C. Williams, artist. Boothbay Harbor, 2010. Richard Cheek, photographer.
30. Garden ornament, motel grounds along U. S. Route 1, north of Rockland, 2010. Richard Cheek, photographer.
31. Guest house, Sebasco Harbor Resort, Sebasco, 2010. Richard Cheek, photographer.
32. Lighthouse Lobster Shack at The Maine Heritage Village, U. S. Route 1, south of Wiscasset, 2010. Richard Cheek, photographer.
33. Broadbay Electric sign, State Route 90, west of West Rockport, 2010. Richard Cheek, photographer.
34. Acadia Fuel propane tank, State Route 3, Trenton, 2010. Richard Cheek, photographer.
35. Mid-Coast Auto Sales sign, U. S. Route 1, southwest of Rockland, 2010. Richard Cheek, photographer.
36. Pottle Realty Group sign, State Route 26, south of Boothbay, 2010. Richard Cheek, photographer.
37. Midcoast Federal Credit Union sign, U. S. Route 1, southwest of Rockland, 2010. Richard Cheek, photographer.
38. Maine Coast Stove and Chimney Company sign, U. S. Route 1, south of Wiscasset, 2010. Richard Cheek, photographer.
39. Ship's wheel-shaped souvenir dish depicting Portland Head Light, c. 1900. Justin Goodstein-Aue, photographer. Promised gift to Historic New England.
40. Doorstop with lighthouse and keeper's house, early twentieth century. Justin Goodstein-Aue, photographer. Promised gift to Historic New England.
41. Beer stein depicting Portland Head Light, c. 1890. Andrew Davis, photographer. Promised gift to Historic New England.
42. Painted cast-iron lighthouse model with light, c. 1900. Adam Osgood, photographer. Promised gift to Historic New England.
43. Leaf-shaped souvenir dish depicting Portland Head Light, c. 1900. Andrew Davis, photographer. Promised gift to Historic New England.
44. Bedroom, view with quilt, Little residence, Minneapolis, Minnesota, 2010.
45. Lighthouse statue collection, Allen residence, Voorheesville, New York, 2010.
46. Living room, Grace residence, Watonga, Oklahoma, 2010.
47. Bathroom, Houtman residence, Kalamazoo, Michigan, 2010.
48. Bedroom, Hemstad residence, Milaca, Minnesota, 2010.

49. Bedroom, Kaplan residence, Buena Vista, Georgia, 2010.
50. Front page from *The Southern Maine Coastal Beacon*, August 18–25, 1994. *Lighthouse Digest* archives.
51. Business sign for the Lighthouse Depot Store, U. S. Route 1, Wells, 2010. Richard Cheek, photographer.
52. Michael Kimball, "A Love of Lighthouses," *Yankee*, August 1994. Promised gift to Historic New England.
53. Cover of *Lighthouses of Maine and New Hampshire* by Kathleen E. Finnegan and Timothy E. Harrison. (South Portland, Maine: Lighthouse Digest, 1991.) Promised gift to Historic New England.
54. Pages from Lighthouse Depot catalogue, 2008. Promised gift to Historic New England.
55. Alan Claude, *Portland Head Light*. © Alan Claude 2007. *Portland Head Light* is from graphic artist Alan Claude's Lighthouse Travel Poster Collection, an interpretation of New England lighthouses and their surrounding environments. www.alanclaude.com.

ENDNOTES

1. George Stuyvesant Jackson, *A Maine Heritage: The History of the Union Mutual Life Insurance Company* (Portland, Maine: Union Mutual, 1964), 118.
2. Jackson, *A Maine Heritage*, 195.
3. Kathleen E. Finnegan and Timothy E. Harrison, *Lighthouses of Maine and New Hampshire* (South Portland, Maine: Lighthouse Digest, 1991), [3].
4. Michael Kimball, "A Love of Lighthouses," *Yankee*, August 1994, 23.
5. Cover slogan for Lighthouse Depot catalogues in 2010 and 2011.

ADDITIONAL RESOURCES

Jackson, George Stuyvesant. *A Maine Heritage: The History of the Union Mutual Life Insurance Company*. Portland, Maine: Union Mutual Life Insurance Company, 1964.
Harrison, Timothy E. *Portland Head Light: The Grand Daddy of All Lighthouses*. Wells, Maine: FogHorn Publishing, 2006.

Special thanks go to Don Devine of the Lighthouse Depot in Wells and Ludolf and Ruth Ann Bierwas of By the Bay Lighthouses in Searsport for their insights regarding the creation and marketing of all forms of lighthouse-related merchandise.

Saving the Sentinels
The Preservation of Maine's Light Stations

ILLUSTRATION SOURCES

1. Light tower/keeper's house, Egg Rock Light Station, Winter Harbor, 1992. Richard Cheek, photographer.
2. Restoration of Portland Head Light, 2005. Timothy Harrison, photographer. *Lighthouse Digest* archives.
3. American Lighthouse Foundation patch. Maine Lighthouse Museum, Rockland.
4. United States Lighthouse Society logo. United States Lighthouse Society.
5. Lighthouse Preservation Society logo. Lighthouse Preservation Society.
6. Ken Black, 1992. Peter Ralston, photographer. Maine Lighthouse Museum, Rockland.
7. Poster for the Lighthouse Conference, Maine's Lighthouses: Preservation Challenges and Solutions, October 18–20, 1985. Maine Historic Preservation Commission.
8. Light tower and fog signal station, Libby Island Light Station, Machiasport, 1991. Richard Cheek, photographer.
9. Boathouse, view west southwest, Petit Manan Light Station, Milbridge, 1990. Richard Cheek, photographer. Library of Congress, Prints and Photographs Division, HABS ME,15–MILB.V,2–8.

10. Bell tower, Perkin's Island Light Station, Georgetown, 1989. Richard Cheek, photographer. Library of Congress, Prints and Photographs Division, HABS ME,12–GEOTO,1–6.
11. Heron Neck Light, c. 1889. Henry Peabody, photographer. Historic New England Library and Archives.
12. Newspaper clipping reporting the fire at Heron Neck Light, from the *Coastal Maine Courier-Gazette*, May 2, 1989. Maine Historic Preservation Commission.
13. Vignette of Heron Neck Light from *The Coast of Maine*, 1889. Historic New England Library and Archives.
14. Heron Neck Light after restoration. Christine Morton, photographer. *Lighthouse Digest* archives.
15. "Heron Neck Rescue," from *Lighthouse Digest*, May 1992. *Lighthouse Digest* archives.
16. The framed walkway at Goat Island Light Station, 2011. Courtesy of Scott and Karen Dombroski, Kennebunkport Conservation Trust.
17. Restoration of the Goat Island bell tower. Courtesy of Scott and Karen Dombroski, Kennebunkport Conservation Trust.
18. Doubling Point Light tower being hoisted back into place after restoration, January 2000. Kathleen Finnegan, photographer. *Lighthouse Digest* archives.
19. Restoration work at West Quoddy Light Station. Timothy Harrison, photographer. *Lighthouse Digest* archives.
20. The inside of the Fresnel lens at Seguin Light Station after restoration. Jeremy D'Entremont, photographer. *Lighthouse Digest* archives.
21. Boy Scouts painting the house at Little River Light Station, 2006. Courtesy of the Friends of Little River Lighthouse, a chapter of the American Lighthouse Foundation.
22. Sunrise over Egg Rock Light Station, 2006. Richard Cheek, photographer.
23. "Save the Lighthouse" button. *Lighthouse Digest* archives.

PRINCIPAL RESOURCES

Inventory of Historic Light Stations. Washington, D. C.: National Maritime Initiative, National Park Service, History Division, 1994.
Lighthouse files, Maine Historic Preservation Commission, Augusta, Maine.
Maine Lighthouse Selection Committee Manual. Material related to the Maine Lights Program selection process.

Back Matter Illustrations

PAGE 222: Lighthouse Brand label, c. 1900. Promised gift to Historic New England.
PAGE 225: Paperweight depicting Wood Island Light, c. 1920. Justin Goodstein-Aue, photographer. Promised gift to Historic New England.
PAGE 227: Chewing gum card depicting the signal pennant of the Lighthouse Service, Pennant Gum Company, Philadelphia, early twentieth century. Promised gift to Historic New England.
PAGE 228: Cover of *The Watchers on the Longships: A Tale of Cornwall in the Last Century* by James Cobb. (London: Wells Gardner, Darton, and Company, 1899). Private collection.
PAGE 231: Page from an unidentified alphabet book, early twentieth century. *Lighthouse Digest* archives.
PAGE 233: Cover of *Lighthouses on Parade, Portland, Maine: A Community Art Project Presented by Hannaford*. (Rochester, N. Y.: Monroe Litho, 2003). Promised gift to Historic New England.
PAGE 240: Souvenir plate depicting Spring Point Light, c. 1900. Justin Goodstein-Aue, photographer. Promised gift to Historic New England.

Index

PUBLISHED BY HISTORIC NEW ENGLAND

141 Cambridge Street
Boston, Massachusetts 02114
www.HistoricNewEngland.org

DISTRIBUTED BY TILBURY HOUSE, PUBLISHERS

103 Brunswick Avenue
Gardiner, Maine 04345
www.tilburyhouse.com
800-582-1899

FIRST EDITION 2012

Library of Congress Cataloging-in-Publication Data
From guiding lights to beacons for business : the many lives of
Maine's lighthouses / edited by Richard Cheek ; introduction by
Olympia J. Snowe.
    p. cm.
"With essays by W. H. Bunting, Richard Cheek, Thomas Andrew
Denenberg, Timothy Harrison, Kirk F. Mohney, David Richards,
and Earle G. Shettleworth, Jr."
Includes bibliographical references and index.
ISBN 978-0-88448-338-0 (pbk. : alk. paper)
1. Lighthouses—Maine—History. I. Cheek, Richard.
VK1024.M2F76 2012
387.1'5509741—dc23
                2012013142

Book and cover design by Julia Sedykh Design
Printed and bound in China by C&C Offset Printing Co., Ltd.

FRONT COVER:
Keeper's house, light tower, and bell house, view east, Bass Harbor
    Light Station, Bass Harbor, 1990. Richard Cheek, photographer.
Union Mutual Life Insurance Company newsletter letterhead,
    February–March 1899. Maine Historic Preservation Commission.
Label for Jonesport Fancy Clams, c. 1920. R. B. & C. G. Stevens
    Company, Jonesport. Promised gift to Historic New England.

BACK COVER:
Greeting card printed with the message "Do Good," late nineteenth
    century. Promised gift to Historic New England.

FRONT INSIDE COVER:
Postcard of Nubble Light, York, c. 1910. Hugh C. Leighton Company,
    publishers. Maine Historic Preservation Commission.

BACK INSIDE COVER:
Postcard of Portland Head Light, Cape Elizabeth, c. 1910. Hugh
    C. Leighton Company, publishers. Maine Historic Preservation
    Commission.

FRONT FLAP:
Souvenir pen, Mauchline ware, depicting Nubble Light, c. 1900.
    Photograph by Justin Goodstein-Aue. Promised gift to Historic
    New England.
Envelope with First Day of Issue stamp, West Quoddy Head Light,
    1990. *Lighthouse Digest* archives.
Envelope with First Day of Issue stamp, ". . . from sea to shining sea,"
    1981. *Lighthouse Digest* archives.
Maine Statehood First Day of Issue stamp, 1970. *Lighthouse Digest*
    archives.
Portland Head Light stamp from the "Maine Vacationland" stamp
    album, 1940. State of Maine Publicity Bureau, publisher. Maine
    Historic Preservation Commission.
Postage stamp, "Greetings from Maine," 2002. *Lighthouse Digest*
    archives.

BACK FLAP:
Cover of the brochure "Portland, Maine: Playground Metropolis,"
    1930s. Maine Historic Preservation Commission.
Cover of the brochure "Vacationland: An Illustrated Register of
    Hotels and Camps in Maine and New Hampshire," 1921. The
    Resort Proprietors and Passenger Traffic Department and Maine
    Central Railroad, publishers. Promised gift to Historic New
    England.
Souvenir matchbook cover featuring Portland Head Light, Diamond
    Match Company, c. 1930. Promised gift to Historic New England.
Cover of *Maine: The Summer Playground of the Nation, The Land
    of Smiling Skies*, c. 1920. Promised gift to Historic New England.
Souvenir spoon, sterling silver, depicting Portland Head Light,
    c. 1900. Photograph by Justin Goodstein-Aue. Promised gift to
    Historic New England.